The Sidewalks of St. Louis

The Sidewalks

Places, People, and Politics

University of Missouri Press • Columbia and London

# of St. Louis

in an American City

George Lipsitz

Copyright © 1991 by
The Curators of the University of Missouri
University of Missouri Press, Columbia, Missouri 65201
Printed and bound in the United States of America
All rights reserved
5 4 3 2 1   95 94 93 92 91

Library of Congress Cataloging-in-Publication Data

Lipsitz, George.
    The sidewalks of St. Louis : places, people, and politics in an
American city / George Lipsitz.
        p.   cm.
    Includes bibliographical references and index.
    ISBN 0–8262–0814–2 (alk. paper)
    1. Saint Louis (Mo.)—Civilization. 2. Saint Louis (Mo.)
—Politics and government. I. Title. II. Title: Sidewalks of Saint Louis.
F474.S25L57   1991
977.8′65—dc20   91–26819
                                                                      CIP

∞™ This paper meets the requirements of the
American National Standard for Permanence of Paper
for Printed Library Materials, Z39.48, 1984.

Designer: Kristie Lee
Typesetter: Connell-Zeko Type & Graphics
Printer: Thomson-Shore, Inc.
Binder: Thomson-Shore, Inc.
Typeface: Antique Olive and Palatino

Photos appearing on part-title pages, top to bottom: Places—State Historical Society of Missouri, Columbia; Western Historical Manuscript Collection, University of Missouri–St. Louis; Missouri Historical Society; People—State Historical Society of Missouri, Columbia; Missouri Historical
Society; Missouri Historical Society; Politics—Western Historical Manuscript Collection, University of Missouri–St. Louis; Missouri Historical
Society, Missouri Historical Society.

to Katharine Corbett

Contents

Politics

The Sidewalks of St. Louis

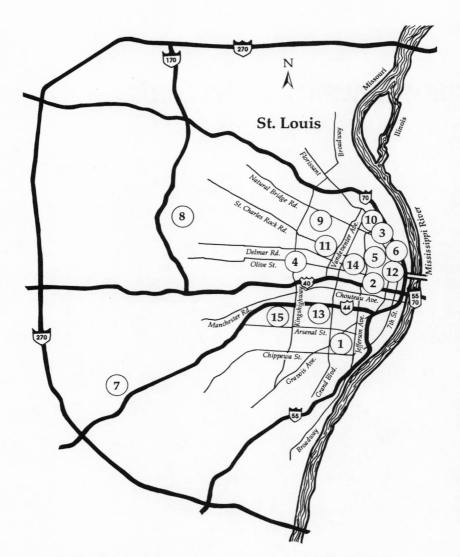

1. Sugarloaf Mound
2. Chouteau's Pond
3. Biddle Street
4. Forest Park
5. Soccer Fields
6. Polish Falcons Hall
7. Meramec Highlands
8. University City
9. Homer G. Phillips Hospital
10. von der Ahe Store
11. Chopin Home
12. Eads Bridge
13. The Grove
14. The Buder Bath (#5)
15. The Hill

Introduction
An Unconventional History

History books about cities generally proceed in chronological order. They trace the development and progress of metropolitan areas from humble beginnings to splendid maturity. In the process, they honor founding families, celebrate the accomplishments of business leaders, and chronicle the careers of politicians. Such books have their uses. Some, like James Neal Primm's study of St. Louis, *The Lion of the Valley,* provide indispensable insight and information. But these conventional urban histories do too little to explore the vital textures of urban life; they are poorly suited for capturing the complex and contradictory processes that make a city.

This is not a conventional urban history. Instead, it is an attempt to reveal the vital textures of urban life by exploring some of the sedimented memories and residual practices that have influenced life and culture in one American city. If you know St. Louis well, you may not recognize the place described here as the one you know. The oft-told stories of architectural landmarks, local heroes, and politics at the center do not appear here. My chapters on places omit the Gateway Arch and the Wainwright Building, my portraits of people ignore Pierre Laclede and Charles Lindbergh, my descriptions of politics neglect Carl Schurz and Raymond Tucker. But all histories make choices about what to include and what to exclude; my hope is that by looking at what might appear to be the margins of life in St. Louis we can learn about a collective past that escapes notice in more conventional accounts. Part of my perspective is that there are many possible ways to tell the story of the city, and I offer this as one of those possibilities. My account is objective in the sense that everything presented in it as fact has been researched as carefully as possible to conform with documentary evidence, but it is not neutral; it has a point of view. It argues for a certain conception of the urban past. It is not comprehensive and does not aim to be. Indeed, the goal of making one big story out of many small ones has led urban historians to concentrate on the narrow experiences of a minute portion of the population, those whose names appear in newspapers and who leave their personal papers to archival collections, and to all but ignore the histories of the majority of the population past and present. This not only makes for flawed history, but it also has dangerous political ramifications for the present where, all too often, the narrowly focused best interests of elites are presented as synonymous with the welfare of entire cities.

Cities abound with conflict and argument. They draw their absorbing energy and compelling dynamism from difference, diversity, and division. Judgments about urban life are perspectival: one person's progress can bring destruction to someone else; what some people see as decay or blight, others might treasure as tradition. To present urban history as a unified story told from one point of view distorts the past and decreases our ability to understand the present. Too often, urban histories treat cities as corporate entities, as if everyone in them had the same interests and goals. Worse yet, some urban histories treat places as organic entities with prearranged destinies interrupted only by nonhuman phenomena like "blight" or "decay." In my view cities are created by human activity and everything that happens in them can be traced to human agency. The city of St. Louis forms my object of study not because I think it has innate destiny or immutable character, but rather because it has been an interesting crossroads that has benefited from the currents of mind and spirit flowing through it.

The problem of the city is the problem of difference. The city's physical enclosures force people to confront one another, to recognize the existence of different classes and different races, of different interests and different tastes. As a stage for such confrontations, the city often takes on a menacing presence in the popular imagination. Our culture presents few positive and many negative images of the city. Popular culture's images of the city usually emphasize its dangers and divisions. Government policies generally work toward the regulation and control of the city; they promise to "clean up the mess" and restore order. But the city is also the site of mutuality and reciprocity, the locus of "politics" in the best sense of the word. It is the place where people see their destinies as interdependent, where they fashion institutions for mutual advancement, and where collective imagination and effort create new possibilities.

This is a book about the history of St. Louis, but it is also intended as a brief on behalf of city life, an argument in favor of its accidents and surprises. It proceeds from the assumption that people know more collectively than they know as individuals, and that the best societies are those that draw the broadest possible participation from their citizens. Conventional urban histories with their unified narratives told from one point of view contain some truth. But theirs is not the only truth, just the most familiar. In this book, I present some other truths, some other stories about the places, people, and politics of St. Louis. These are not stories about progress and growth; they do not focus on the city's first families, or its business and political leaders. Instead, they examine the legacy left to the city by its accidents and improvisations. They explore the lives of oddballs and outcasts, immigrants and artists, women and workers, and many of those whose influence is rarely acknowledged in the standard histories.

The truths in this book are compelling to me because I have lived them. I know their influence on my own life. I have come to see that no matter how suppressed or silenced these urban memories may have become, they hold the power to free us to love and to help and to learn from one another.

*   *   *

I first came to St. Louis in 1963. I traveled from my home in Paterson, New Jersey to attend the American Freedom Summer Institute for high school students at Washington University. The next year, I enrolled as a freshman at Washington University and stayed in the city with only short interruptions until 1982. I received a wonderful education in St. Louis, only part of it in the classroom. It was from the city itself that much of my learning came, from the places, people, and politics that I encountered there.

From my dormitory at Washington University I could walk west through Clayton and Ladue, two of the wealthiest suburbs in the nation. If I went north and east, I walked through racially mixed working-class shopping strips near the Wellston Loop and along what was then Easton Avenue (now Martin Luther King Boulevard). By walking across Skinker Boulevard, I entered Forest Park with its free zoo, art museum, and walking paths. A Bi-State bus would take me along Goodfellow Boulevard and St. Louis Avenue through wonderful tree-lined black neighborhoods teeming with a vibrant street life to old Busch Stadium at Grand and Dodier. Another bus would deliver me to Cherokee Street, to a neighborhood filled with country-and-western record stores, secondhand furniture shops, and people whose accents marked them as migrants from the Ozarks and the Missouri Bootheel region.

Part of my education about St. Louis came through the radio. At one end of the dial I heard Skeets Yaney play country-and-western music; he always introduced himself with his theme song "Back Home Again in Indiana." At the other end of the dial, disc jockeys Lou "Father" Thimes and Mitchell Hearns "Gabriel" played jazz and blues. On Saturday afternoons, they'd promise to "go into the basement and open up a bucket of nails," which meant they were about to play nothing but the blues. In between those stations, a south St. Louis Italian-American calling himself Johnny Rabbit, accompanied by his imaginary companion Bruno J. Grunion, played "top forty" rock and roll. During daytime hours, a Festus station broadcast the country-gospel music of Don and Earl, who offered their listeners the opportunity to purchase items including "miracle" pictures of Jesus that appeared in the sky after you stared at them, and the *Post Rapture Journal*, the newspaper that they felt would be published the day after Armageddon.

Excursions into the city and eclectic sampling from the radio introduced me to the diversity of St. Louis, but my increasing political activism taught me about the serious issues underlying these surface appearances. A campus civil rights group working with the St. Louis chapter of the Congress of Racial Equality mobilized volunteers to do voter registration for the 1964 elections. We went door-to-door in the all-black St. Louis County suburb of Kinloch where we encountered a degree of poverty that I had never seen before outside the rural South. Even more shocking were our afternoons canvassing at the Pruitt-Igoe housing project in north St. Louis. As someone who grew up in a decaying industrial city, I was no stranger to poverty; from the time I was in the third grade I had playmates who lived in public housing projects. But I had never seen anything like Pruitt-Igoe, with its elevators that stopped only on every third floor and its dark narrow stairwells and hallways that looked like they had been designed expressly for crime. But more frightening than the strange design and obviously poor construction (including exposed hot water pipes) was the palpable rage simmering among the residents of the buildings. Very few people wanted to answer their doors, and not many of those who did felt like talking about voter registration. To us, as middle-class college students, voting seemed like an important way to influence what happened in society. But most of the people we talked with at Pruitt-Igoe made it clear that they had no faith in such measures. It took me some time and a lot of education about conditions in the inner city to understand what they meant. But their anger and the conditions in which they lived left a lasting impression on me. I found that I couldn't push them from my mind even when I tried.

The mid–1960s were a frightening time for St. Louis and for American society in general. As Americans and Vietnamese squared off in mortal combat halfway around the globe, American cities faced an unprecedented eruption of violence on the home front. Police officers and vigilantes brutalized civil rights demonstrators in both the North and South. Ghetto insurrections destroyed millions of dollars worth of property and provoked a level of repression that left thousands wounded and hundreds dead. In St. Louis, tensions between police officers and citizens escalated in repeated instances of violence. Police officers shot six black suspects in the back during the summer of 1965, three in one week. The cumulative effects of urban renewal and flight by industry and investors left the city with severe problems, including high levels of unemployment, shortages of adequate affordable housing, a decaying industrial and commercial infrastructure, dreadful levels of infant mortality and lead poisoning among children, and severe declines in city services. Mobilization by civil rights activists and the first faltering steps of the War on Poverty called attention to the dire conditions in the city, but polarization between whites and blacks and between the rich and the poor effectively frustrated any meaningful effort to solve urban problems.

Yet in those frightening times, St. Louis offered important lessons, and not just negative ones. For in the face of all these painful changes and struggles there were always human beings working to preserve the gains of the past and to help build a decent and humane city in the future. In the city's churches and schools and community centers I found people whose histories positioned them for a critical stance in the present, and in and around the city's schools I met many of their children. Some were the offspring of solidly middle-class European ethnics who brought their families' collective memory into discussions at Roosevelt and Cleveland and Southwest high schools. Others were the children of those displaced by urban renewal, descendants of migrants from the rural South whose racial and class perspectives shaped their discussions with me at Northwest and Sumner and Soldan high schools.

I worked for underground and community newspapers, in and around dozens of political projects. I learned about rank-and-file caucuses in the Teamsters and Transit Workers unions during discussions with workers in their north and south side houses. Their experiences were very different from mine—most had dropped out of high school, served in the military, and gone to work at wage labor jobs that they expected to hold for their whole lives. But when we swapped stories about bureaucrats, those in the military and those in the university sounded very similar. When we sat up and listened to music by Roberta Flack or Merle Haggard we found that attachments to popular culture transcended class and racial lines. The anger and aspirations of women factory workers were not very different from those I heard from middle-class feminists. Of course there were divisive moments and awkward differences, but these too were valuable to all of us in figuring out the problems of the city and our responses to them.

One day we heard about a strike by women workers at a bank in Baden, the German neighborhood on the far northern edge of the city. A woman in the rank-and-file Teamster caucus, a clerk at a drug company, started telephoning her friends to ask them to join the picket line in Baden. The next afternoon, from 4:00 to 6:00 P.M. on a workday, a picket line of over one hundred people—blacks, whites, men, women, workers, students, professionals—demonstrated solidarity with the strike. A black worker at the Coca-Cola Bottling Plant in far south St. Louis drove all the way up to Baden at the end of his shift to join that picket line on behalf of workers he didn't know in a neighborhood where he had every reason to feel unwelcome. Our numbers, our diversity, and our ability to find common purpose made that day special, not only because of the direct material aid it brought to the strikers, but also because it demonstrated to each of us the potential and power of the idea of community. We lost most of the battles we fought, at least in the short run, but even while losing we succeeded in maintaining a very precious legacy of political action and social solidarity.

The Nixon administration's curtailment of funds for public housing and its abandonment of the War on Poverty in 1973 coincided with a serious recession that had devastating effects on St. Louis, as it did on urban areas all across the country. Federal revenue sharing diverted money away from the poor in order to cut real estate taxes for businesses and wealthy individuals, while financiers demanded austerity measures from city governments as a condition of continued credit, a demand that effectively transferred millions of dollars of capital from public to private uses. For those most dependent upon city services, these decisions meant disastrous cuts in necessary health, housing, and educational programs, exacerbating the chasm between classes and races while turning public services into inadequate institutions of last resort, which were utilized mostly by only the most desperate and most forgotten sectors of the population.

During these years I witnessed the devastation of the city first-hand. Political activism brought me in contact with desperate families, parents whose children suffered from the unchecked epidemic of lead poisoning among poor youths and those who could not find shelter on the private market at a price they could afford. I talked with homeowners facing financial disaster because highway construction or other forms of urban renewal threatened to undermine the equity they had established in their houses. Within the trade union movement I saw caucuses of rank-and-file workers mobilizing against management speed-ups and union collaboration with management as the city's declining industrial base enabled employers to exact ever-greater concessions from labor. As a teacher at the University of Missouri–St. Louis, I saw firsthand the nervous anxiety and intermittent rage of white and black working-class students hoping that an education would provide them with upward mobility while at the same time observing the ways in which de-industrialization was diminishing opportunities and resources within their own families and neighborhoods.

Like me, many of these people had come to love St. Louis, not in spite of its history, but rather, because of it. What made living in the city still bearable was its inheritance from the past—its wonderful parks built because of the idealism and civic-mindedness of nineteenth-century liberal reformers, its magnificent libraries and art museums established at a time when universal access to education and art seemed like a civic responsibility, and its eclectic and beautiful architecture fashioned from the hard labor and inspired imagination of immigrant craftsmen and women.

The many layers of the city's past made themselves manifest in innumerable ways. On cold winter days when you ice-skated in Forest Park or on hot summer nights when you sat in Bellerive Park and listened for calliopes on the riverboats, you used resources saved for you by farsighted people from the past. You absorbed the resonance of the past on a hot June day at a south side church's Croatian picnic, where they cooked Italian sausages and danced to German polkas, or when you walked down Martin Luther King Boulevard and heard Jackie Wilson singing "Danny Boy" coming from a jukebox, while you smelled the aromas of chitlins and collard greens cooking at soul food restaurants that were located next door to pawnshops owned by older white European immigrants. At rock and roll nightclubs, rural whites and middle-class ethnics went wild every time the band played the boogie-woogie shuffle rhythms of Chuck Berry, Ike Turner, and other great St. Louis black musicians. For all the somber costs of difference registered in prejudice, parochialism, and conflict, the diversity of the city was its greatest strength, and the increasing erasure of it by redevelopment and segregation its greatest tragedy.

Not much of this tragedy seemed evident to St. Louis's political and business elites or to their allies in the media. To them, the history of St. Louis was a burden that could be lifted only through energetic action by bulldozers and construction crews. They lauded the destruction of inner-city neighborhoods and the growth of the suburbs. Inside the city limits, they demanded lavish tax-supported subsidies for corporate office buildings, fancy restaurants, and luxury apartments. They systematically disassembled the downtown and the riverfront to make it attractive to tourists and outside investors. They replaced the downtown's decentralized commercial districts, whose streets vibrated with the energies of mixed uses, with suburban-styled shopping malls and surrounded the downtown with a buffer zone of evacuated neighborhoods, abandoned buildings and empty streets.

Renovation and urban renewal in St. Louis took aim at the treasured legacy of the past. But however destructive these policies have been, however insidious their influence on the physical form and political culture of the city, they have not succeeded in purging the past from St. Louis. I remember a discussion with a museum curator, a sophisticated professional woman with an advanced educational degree and what seemed to me to be an affluent lifestyle. She told me that she supported the players in the 1981 baseball strike, explaining that when she was growing up in suburban St. Louis County her father sometimes took her back to his boyhood Soulard neighborhood on the near south side. She remembers he once showed her a spot that his father had showed him, a former smelting mill where a worker had to have his feet amputated because molten steel spilled on them. The moral of the story told across the generations was that workers had no protection without unions and that employers would do anything they could get away with. Another time, a white Bulgarian-American warehouse worker explained to me in great detail why black nationalism was a good thing. He told me that when he was growing up in one of the small industrial cities on the Illinois side of the Mississippi River he remembered when his parents started feeling ashamed of their ethnic past, and how they stopped reading the foreign language press in an effort to prove themselves "one hundred percent" American in the wake of the xenophobia brought on by the anti-communist hysteria of the early 1950s. He told me that he did not know how it felt to be black, but he did understand how awful it was for the dominant culture to make you feel ashamed of yourself because of your ancestral identity.

I never wanted to leave St. Louis. After receiving my master's degree from the University of Missouri–St. Louis, I did my Ph.D. work at the University of Wisconsin because it seemed to me to be the school closest to St. Louis that offered the kind of degree most likely to make me employable after graduate school. While finishing my degree, I taught again at the University of Missouri–St. Louis for two years, but in 1979 I got a full-time job at the University of Houston at Clear Lake City, Texas. The next year, I resigned my tenure track job in Houston to return to a totally precarious job at the University of Missouri–St. Louis trying to set up a St. Louis History Institute. I had no job security in that position, and worked full time for $12,000 a year. When catastrophic budget cuts slashed the university's resources, I tried to hang on to that post at a reduced salary, offering to work for $8,000. But when I was informed that the school could not afford me at even that salary, I reapplied for my old job in Houston, was rehired, and left St. Louis for good.

In the month when I made my painful last departure from St. Louis, my former teacher and colleague at the University of Missouri–St. Louis, Charles Korr, put me in touch with Greg Holzauer, then the managing editor of *St. Louis* magazine. He had been looking for someone to write an ongoing feature for that publication on local history, and Professor Korr suggested me for the job. For the next three years I wrote the "St. Louis Scrapbook" feature for *St. Louis* magazine, which is where most of the entries in this book first appeared. In that role, I tried to convey to St. Louisans how precious their city was, but also how much it was threatened by the economic and social changes of the 1980s. Over the years people have suggested that I collect those columns and publish them separately as a book, which is what I am doing in this volume.

In some of my other writing, notably *A Life in the Struggle: Ivory Perry and the Culture of Opposition* (1988) and in *Discursive Space and Social Place* (forthcoming) I have detailed some of the history of urban redevelopment and its consequences in St. Louis. In this book, I attempt to focus attention on another aspect of St. Louis—its collective memories of solidarity and struggle. The organization of *Sidewalks of St. Louis* tries to replicate the feel of urban life with its many discoveries and ironic contradictions. Yet even if successful, it will not be the last word on St. Louis or on other cities like it.

There are too many problems out there to warrant such a quick termination of discussion; no one can afford the illusion of having had the first or last word in an ongoing dialogue. Instead, I hope that this book will lead to the remembrance and rearticulation of some things that have already been said, to the continuation of a dialogue in which some of the suppressed voices from the past finally get to speak again, and this time, maybe get the chance to be heard and understood.

I am grateful to many people for the things that I have learned from them about urban life. I especially want to thank here some St. Louisans whose attention to the city has added significantly to my knowledge, including Miss Julia Davis, Neal Primm, Bernie Hayes, Linda Kulla, Charles Korr, and the inimitable Onion Horton. Foremost among this group is Katharine Corbett of the Missouri Historical Society. Over the past ten years she has transformed both popular and academic reflections on St. Louis history by asking the right questions in the right ways. Her efforts demonstrate how intellectual work can be shared by an entire community, and her accomplishments set a new standard for historical inquiry. This book is dedicated to her with deep appreciation and respect, because she knows how important history is and because she knows how to do it well.

Old Rock House

Photo: Missouri Historical
Society

The Old Rock House tavern
was a popular hangout for
Jack Conroy and many of the
other WPA writers and artists
in St. Louis in the 1930s.

The Rosebud Bar

Photo: Missouri Historical Society

Tom Turpin's Rosebud Bar served as a central meeting place for St. Louis's ragtime musicians at the turn of the century. This advertisement appeared in the *St. Louis Palladium* on January 16, 1904. The state of Missouri and the city of St. Louis have recently earmarked more than $1.3 million to turn Scott Joplin's St. Louis residence into a museum and to build a replica of the Rosebud Bar next door.

129 Market Street

Photo: National Park Service,
Jefferson National Expansion
Memorial

This interior of a Market
Street saloon was photo-
graphed in 1938 as part of a
project to document the inte-
riors of buildings slated for
destruction by land clearance
for the Gateway Arch and
Jefferson National Expansion
Memorial along the river-
front.

W. C. Handy

Photo: Missouri Historical
Society

A portrait taken inside the
Old Rock House when an
elderly W. C. Handy (seated
with cane) visited St. Louis,
the inspiration for his most
famous song.

Chouteau's Pond
Photo: Missouri Historical Society

This daguerreotype, taken in 1851, shows a view of the drained area of Chouteau's Pond. The pond played an important role in the early economic growth of the city and divided the city into north and south sides. Its use as a dumping site for refuse and waste made the pond a health hazard, and it had to be drained after the city's disastrous mid-century cholera epidemic. Yet even after the pond no longer existed, the divisions that it imposed on the city remained.

Jahn Statue
Photo: Missouri Historical
Society

This statue in Forest Park
honors the father of physical
culture and the founder of the
Turnvereins.

St. Louis Turn Halle
Photo: Missouri Historical
Society

Turn Halle at 1508 Chouteau
Avenue, meeting place of the
Turnvereins, ca. 1900.

Turnverein Gymnasts
Photo: Missouri Historical
Society

At a time when public parks
and playgrounds provided
few opportunities for recreation, fraternal orders like the
Turnvereins and the Polish
Falcons offered gymnastic
and sporting facilities for
their members.

Black Club Women
Photo: Western Historical Manuscript Collection, University of Missouri-St. Louis

In 1900, St. Louis ranked second to Baltimore among major cities in its percentage of African-American residents. The black community in St. Louis established many institutions of national and international importance, including Sumner High School, Poro Beauty College, and Homer G. Phillips Hospital. Building these institutions required leadership and coordination from many groups, including these club women.

Championship Soccer Match
Photo: Missouri Historical Society

A championship soccer match between St. Louis's Stix, Baer & Fuller Football Club and the New York Americans Football Club. In certain sections of St. Louis, the "big game" has always been soccer.

International Athletes
Photo: Missouri Historical Society

Competitors in the marathon at the 1904 St. Louis Olympics. Felix Carvajal of Cuba (second from left) is wearing the beret and street shoes.

200-Meter Hurdle Race
Photo: Missouri Historical Society

At the 1904 Olympics, held in St. Louis, George Poage won the silver medal in the 200-meter hurdles and became the first black medal winner in the modern Olympics.

Red and Whitey
Photo: David Rae Morris

Hall-of-Famer Red Schoen-
dienst and Cardinals' manager Whitey Herzog discuss
matters before a 1990 game
in Los Angeles. Professional
baseball enjoyed its initial
success in St. Louis as part
of a promotional strategy for
selling beer, and it resumed
that role in 1953 when the
Cardinals were purchased by
the Anheuser-Busch Corporation. Schoendienst played for
the Cardinals from 1945 to
1956 and from 1961 to 1963.
He managed the club from
1965 to 1976, while Herzog
managed the team from 1980
to 1990.

Virginia Minor

Photo: Western Historical Manuscript Collection, University of Missouri-St. Louis

Virginia Minor filed suit in a St. Louis federal court, arguing that denying women the vote denied them equal protection of the law. The Supreme Court ruled against her in 1875, but Minor's efforts played an important role in building the movement for women's suffrage that finally succeeded with the passage of a constitutional amendment shortly after World War I.

Kate Chopin

Photo: Missouri Historical Society

An 1893 portrait of Kate Chopin, author of *The Awakening*.

Family Portrait

Photo: Missouri Historical Society

Kate Chopin poses with four of her children.

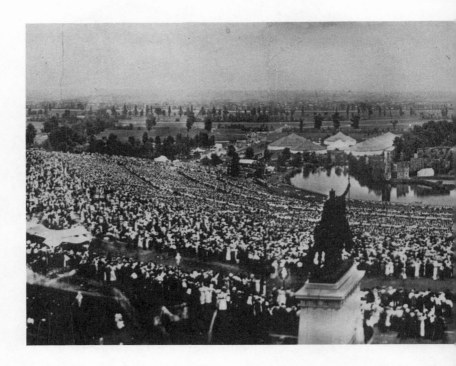

Panoramic View of the Pageant and Masque

Photo: Missouri Historical Society

A panoramic view of the crowd assembled on Art Hill in Forest Park, under the statue of St. Louis, to watch the performance of the Pageant and Masque on stages erected on the lagoons below.

Planning the Pageant and Masque
Photo: Missouri Historical Society

Percy MacKaye, Joseph Linden Smith, and Thomas Wood Stephens (left to right) with a model of the stage for the Pageant and Masque in Forest Park.

Sumner High School

Photo: Western Historical Manuscript Collection, University of Missouri-St. Louis

Throughout the nineteenth century, black St. Louisans struggled for access to public education. Among their accomplishments was the establishment of Sumner High School, the first high school for blacks west of the Mississippi River.

Sumner High School Class

Photo: Western Historical Manuscript Collection, University of Missouri-St. Louis

Students study in a Sumner High School classroom.

Homer G. Phillips Hospital
Photo: Missouri Historical Society

For black St. Louisans, Homer G. Phillips Hospital has not only served as an all-purpose medical facility, but also as a symbol of promises secured and implemented through political struggle.

Baths and Bathers at the Ashley
Photo: Missouri Historical Society

A group of bathers outside a settlement house bath early in the century.

Biddle Street Market
Photo: Missouri Historical Society

A Biddle Street market in the 1920s. Biddle Street is only twenty-six blocks long, but a lot of St. Louis's history has revolved around it.

Scullin Steel Company
Photo: Karen Elshout, *St. Louis Post-Dispatch*

Scullin Steel on Manchester Avenue was just one of the many factories in St. Louis to shut its doors in the 1980s. This sign has been donated to the history museum in Forest Park, and a developer plans to convert the factory grounds into a shopping center.

Places

Sugarloaf Mound: Burying the Past

Sugarloaf Mound in the 4400 block of Ohio Avenue is one of St. Louis's most important historic sites. Although it may look like just another unimposing little patch of grass and dirt, it constitutes the last standing physical remnant within the city limits of centuries-old Native American settlements in the region.

Few people think of St. Louis as a place where Indians lived. For some reason the last three hundred years of Spanish, French, and American occupation seem more like "history" than the 10,000 to 20,000 years of Native American history and culture that preceded it. But long before the first European explorers set foot in North America, St. Louis served as an important center of one of the world's most advanced civilizations—the Mississippian Indians.

At a time when most parts of Europe lacked both the agricultural surplus and the political sophistication necessary for the establishment of large cities, more than forty thousand Native Americans lived in peace and harmony just a few miles east of St. Louis in what is now Cahokia, Illinois. In the thirteenth century, Cahokia had more residents than London. This society employed sophisticated agricultural techniques, developed complex political structures, and displayed great prowess in art and architecture. They covered the area in which they lived with huge mounds which served as ceremonial, burial, and surveillance sites, motivating later generations of settlers to refer to them as the "mound builders."

Mississippian Indian burial mounds served as resting places for the dead, but they also contained the tools and domestic utensils of the deceased. Like many preindustrial peoples, the mound builders recognized only a fine line between life and afterlife, and they did their best to placate the spirits of the dead by keeping one's possessions in life near his or her remains in death. These practices demonstrated honor and respect for the dead, and they forced the living to acknowledge their connection to a long history of growth and decay that superseded the concerns of any one life.

At one time, at least twenty-five huge mounds dotted the terrain on the west side of the Mississippi River. The "Great Mound" on what is now Mound Street and Broadway so impressed the first French settlers in St. Louis that they named it "*la grange de terre*" (the barn of the earth). For most of the nineteenth century, St. Louisans referred to their home as the "mound city." Captain John O'Fallon wrote with wonder and pride about the mound on his family's estate on Bellefontaine Road in the mid-nineteenth century. Forest

Park remained available for development as park land as late as the 1870s only because its many mounds made commercial or residential development there too costly. Six centuries after the demise of their civilization, the mound builders still exert a powerful influence over the physical appearance of St. Louis.

City fathers leveled the "Great Mound" in 1860 to stimulate commercial development. The World's Fair of 1904 with its attendant construction led to the demolition of the mounds in Forest Park. By 1911, only nine mounds remained within the city limits, and all but one of those have been eliminated in the intervening years without fanfare or apparent regret. Although only a fraction of its former size, Sugarloaf Mound remains the last Indian mound within the city limits.

Why did St. Louisans treat these precious and irreplaceable artifacts of a great civilization with such disdain? One reason might be the inevitable misunderstandings that ensue when one culture confronts another. The anthropologist Sidney Mintz once observed that superstition is some other person's religion, and one can understand why "modern" nineteenth-century St. Louisans saw nothing of value in the mounds. From a business perspective, clay and earth mounds three thousand yards long and two hundred yards wide hardly seemed like an efficient use of real estate. On the contrary, they presented a substantial barrier to orderly development. With some elements of the past already well preserved in the fine collection of mounds in Illinois's Cahokia Mounds Park, St. Louisans could see the destruction of the mounds as the removal of a geographic nuisance without harm to the cause of preservation. Yet one other element played a role in decisions to destroy the mounds, and that factor tells us a great deal about the differences between our culture and that of the mound builders.

In the mid-nineteenth century, Americans adopted new ideas about burying the dead. At that time traditional downtown and churchyard grave sites gave way to suburban "rural cemeteries." No longer thought of as mere places to dispose of dead bodies, cemeteries became object lessons for the living, intended to instruct citizens about their collective duty and destiny. Nineteenth-century cemeteries featured landscaped grounds and grave markers replete with civic symbols, much in the manner of public parks. They invited citizens to contemplate the past and to think of themselves as part of a historical continuity. Most important, they used traditional symbols of empire to link the images of the nation-state to immortality.

In the rural cemetery, Americans adopted the symbols of empire for the tombs of the dead. In place of traditional religious icons like crosses or angels, nineteenth-century cemeteries displayed Egyptian obelisks, Roman laurel wreaths, and Greek columns. These architectural forms proclaimed the importance of empire, and they encouraged individual citizens to measure their own worth by the strength of their nation. Of course, previous generations had used the imagery of the nation-state as well, mostly as a means of demonstrating their fidelity to Divine injunctions to build a Godly community, a "city on a hill." But nineteenth-century Americans increasingly converted religious symbols into props designed to bolster the claims of the nation-state.

The establishment of Bellefontaine Cemetery in 1850 brought the "rural cemetery" to St. Louis. Organized by leading citizens and business owners, it created a "city of the dead," characterized by neat orderly lots decorated with civic symbols. In place of the old graveyards at Third and Market, Jefferson and Washington, and Jefferson and Arsenal, St. Louis now had a burial park, beautifully landscaped, in a suburban setting. It invited the living to contemplate the remains of the dead through the lens of national aspirations for empire.

In that context, removal of Indian burial and ceremonial mounds takes on a different significance. The mound builders sought a kind of immortality too, but they did so by invoking the close relationships between the living and the dead as individuals. In their view, spirits from the past lived on in the present; even the greatest accomplishments of the present could not escape the universal destiny of birth, growth, and decay. The mounds asserted no imperial mission, only the commonality of human experience. The demise of the mound builders' civilization marked it as inferior in the eyes of later generations of Europeans. But to the Native Americans themselves it only played out the inevitable destiny of temporal societies. They never attempted to tower above the constraints of time and nature; rather, they tended to blend harmoniously with them. That was not a perspective that particularly appealed to nineteenth-century Americans intent on gaining immortality by emulating the triumphs of the Greeks, Romans, and Egyptians as well as other imperial cultures and civilizations.

Yet the mounds do have something to teach us. They tell about the unity of the human experience, about the fleeting and transitory nature of governments, and about the arrogance of presenting one manifestation of power as a universal truth. In Sugarloaf Mound (which never having been excavated may or may not have been a burial mound) and in Cahokia Mounds State Park at the Cahokia Mounds Interpretive Center we have the opportunity to contemplate a previous culture's attitude toward death and life. As long as the mounds exist, we have the opportunity to encounter a different philosophy of states and nations, one expressed powerfully by Chief Seattle of the Puget Sound tribes, who warned the federal government in 1855

> When the last Red Man shall have perished, and the memory of my tribe shall have become a myth among the white man, these shores will swarm with the invisible dead of my tribe, and when your children's children think themselves alone in the field, the store, the shop, upon the highway, or in the silence of the pathless woods, they will not be alone. In all the earth there is no place dedicated to solitude. At night when the streets of your cities and villages are silent and you think them deserted, they will throng with the returning hosts that once filled them and still love this beautiful land. The white man will never be alone. Let him be just and deal kindly with my people, for the dead are not powerless. Dead, I say? There is not death. Only a change of worlds.

Chouteau's Pond: St. Louis's Invisible Barrier

In St. Louis, north and south are more than points on the compass. They signify neighborhoods, cultures, and experiences that serve as rallying symbols of identity. For all the justified concern about the barriers between the urban city and its county suburbs, everyone who lives in St. Louis knows that the real divisions in the city are not east-west, but rather north-south. People from Baden may have been to Florissant and St. Charles, but Carondelet usually remains exotic to them. Residents of St. Louis Hills may have set foot in Webster Groves and Fenton, but for most of them Hyde Park could just as well be on the moon. I once even witnessed a shouting match between a devotee of the Steak 'n' Shake drive-in restaurant on Morganford and an admirer of the one on Halls Ferry Circle, each one affirming that their hangout was the best, even though the two buildings and their menus were identical. Physically and culturally, the region's dividing line is Highway 40, not the St. Louis city limits.

Conflict between north and south is rooted in several centuries of St. Louis history. Almost one hundred years before an east-west line on the map separated the city and the county, St. Louisans already perceived serious distinctions between north and south, largely because of the location of one of the city's lesser known landmarks—Chouteau's Pond.

In 1767, Pierre Laclede, the merchant and militia officer who did so much to initiate settlement in St. Louis, purchased a significant piece of property from Joseph Taillon. Located on a creek and equipped with a water mill, the site held potential as a spot for milling flour. Laclede constructed a bigger dam on the creek, and acquired adjoining lands to accommodate the resulting pond. At his death in 1778, Laclede left the dam, pond, and surrounding lands to Auguste Chouteau.

The Chouteau family gradually expanded the size of the pond until it covered more than two miles. The property served the city well, functioning as the site of a most successful flour mill. The French had long ridiculed the quantity of bread available in St. Louis, giving the city the derogatory nickname *Pain Court* (short of bread). But by the nineteenth century, Chouteau's mill emerged as an important center of trade, known for its production of high quality flour.

The pond had other uses as well. St. Louis grew up around it, and residents enjoyed swimming and fishing in the summer and ice skating in the winter. The pond offered a beautiful picnic site, a peaceful oasis in the middle of a cluttered and fast-growing metropolis. Clergymen even used it for full immersion baptism, breaking the ice in winter to do so. Fine homes lined the pond, and its banks shaped the directions of urban growth.

For all its attributes, Chouteau's Pond also created some problems. It provided a barrier against southwestern growth, and it made communication difficult between north and south. Streets, sewers, water mains, and public transportation had to skirt the pond, causing expensive alterations and inefficient delivery of goods and services. Because it was easier to surrender to the imperatives of the pond than to fight them, parallel lines of westward growth from both north and south St. Louis became more feasible than unified growth within the central city.

More immediate danger came from local neglect of the environment. Perhaps because the pond had been artificially created in the first place, city residents assumed that they could use it for any desired purpose. They dumped human and industrial waste into it.

Garbage from residences and unused animal parts from butchers' shops found their way into its waters. Oblivious to the area's poor natural drainage, the citizens allowed this stagnant body of waste-filled water to degenerate into a menace to public health.

A cholera epidemic in 1848–1849 demonstrated the dimensions of the pond's threat to the public health. Almost five thousand people died from cholera in the summer of 1849—one hundred forty-five in one day and seven hundred twenty-two in one week. The bodies mounted so quickly that the dead had to be buried *en masse* in underground grottos. St. Louisans decided to fill in the pond and extend the city's network of underground sewers. The epidemic spelled the end for Chouteau's Pond, although not for the patterns of development that it engendered.

Home builders and wealthy residents wanted to escape any association with the cholera plague, so they avoided the central city in favor of developments in the north, south, and west. Realtor R. S. Elliott, who had responded to the epidemic by complaining that "real estate will sell but slowly, when no one was sure from day to day whether he would ever need more land than enough to bury him," grasped new opportunities by investing in the newly developed suburb of Kirkwood. Elliott and his partners boasted of the "healthful fresh air" in the country as a lure to investors from the city. Similar patterns characterized growth to the north, where relocated businesses from the central city developed their own group of clients and investors eager to leave the city and its problems behind. State and federal subsidies to the Pacific Railroad guaranteed the success of Kirkwood and further accelerated the trend toward east-west expansion rather than north-south consolidation. The need for a rail corridor for both industrial and suburban growth made the now-filled pond a desirable site for the railroad yards that replaced Chouteau's Pond as the city's divider.

Chouteau's Pond also played a part in twentieth-century urban renewal in St. Louis. The poor drainage of the pond and its relation to Mill Creek, which had created it, led to the construction of cheap tenements which served as housing for black laborers in the center of the city. The Mill Creek Valley contained the heart of the St. Louis African-American community for many years. It was the birthplace of Roy Wilkins (later the national leader of the National Association for the Advancement of Colored People), the home of the city's first black Presbyterian congregation, and the scene of many nightspots important in the history of jazz music. Yet its economic marginality, dating back to the days of Chouteau's Pond, made it a slum area designated for urban renewal in the 1950s and 1960s. But just as filling in Chouteau's Pond did not revive the central city, the bulldozing of Mill Creek's housing only accelerated the movement of large numbers of its residents into the north side neighborhoods whose inhabitants were deserting them to move westward. Racial discrimination by realtors and shortages of low-income housing forced Mill Creek exiles into overcrowded and often substandard housing, creating new slums in previously stable neighborhoods.

Bodies of water often shape history. Russian diplomats always seek warm weather ports, while Swiss and Bolivian naval officers have limited opportunities for advancement. But few cities find themselves shaped by a body of water that no longer exists. Real and imagined differences divide north and south in St. Louis, but so does a barrier which disappeared in 1849.

Biddle Street: Twenty-Six Blocks of Diversity and Change

Biddle Street consists of only twenty-six short blocks, but it makes up in historical importance what it lacks in physical distance. On the map it runs from the Mississippi River on the east to Jefferson Avenue on the west, but in the history books it runs all the way back to the early nineteenth century. Along the way, it has been the site of the city's first mansions and its first housing projects. It has given its name to blues songs and to churches. It has been the home of German, Irish, Jewish, Italian, and black communities. Probably no street in St. Louis has compressed so many cultures and so much history into so short a distance.

Originally owned by the Carr, Mullanphy, and Biddle families, the land bordering what is now Biddle Street was first developed when Judge William Carr constructed a "country" mansion there in 1820. He used deed restrictions to prevent other people from building near his land and lowering the value of his property. Carr donated land to the city for Carr Square Park, largely as a means of perpetuating vacant land near his estate. But as early as the 1840s, the area attracted ambitious squatters intent on sharing the Carr family's corner of the world. To further discourage any additional settlement, his family built a high fence around the property in 1842.

In the mid-nineteenth century, Irish immigrants settled on Biddle Street near Sixth Street in what became known as Kerry Patch, and German immigrants clustered in houses around Sixteenth Street. St. Patrick's Church at Sixth and Biddle claimed the city's main Irish congregation, while Germans attended St. Joseph's Church at Eleventh and Biddle. With its fine mansions and primitive alley houses, the area supported an economically and ethnically diverse population. A commercial, residential, and cultural center, Biddle Street boasted proximity to three of the first schools in the city—Jefferson, Carr, and Jackson schools.

During the 1877 general strike, workers from all over the city gathered at Schuler's Hall at Fifth and Biddle to plan strategy and voice their demands. Close to the industry along the riverfront and to the working class neighborhoods that did so much to sustain the strike, Biddle Street assumed the same paramount role in a time of civic insurrection that it had maintained in community life for three decades.

The Irish and the Germans predominated along Biddle Street until the 1890s, though Jews and blacks had already started to inhabit dwellings on the street in significant numbers as early as the 1870s. In 1875, St. Louis's first black Presbyterian church began holding services on Twentieth Street, and in the same year a synagogue on Sixth Street became the focal point of religious life for the area's growing Jewish population. Jewish pushcart vendors and store owners established a thriving business on Biddle Street. By the 1890s, it resembled Chicago's famed Maxwell Street which was well known for its variety of merchants and vendors. Around 1910, the Jews began to move west, and large numbers of Sicilians replaced them as residents and merchants in the neighborhood.

In the 1920s, Biddle Street gained a new identity as the center of black migration from rural areas. Blues musicians like Charley Jordan and Jaydee Short performed in Biddle Street clubs and on streetcorners, and their success attracted other musicians to town. Henry Spaulding immortalized the blues scene on the street in May 1929 when he wrote and recorded the "Biddle Street Blues." All across the country, people heard Spaulding sing "Biddle Street, Biddle Street, is twenty-six blocks long, and these women on Biddle Street won't leave me alone." Those who came for a firsthand look at what Spaulding sang about found a crowded thoroughfare filled with dance halls, "pokena" gambling joints, and an array of taverns featuring the music of the legendary Peetie Wheatstraw and the piano wizard Rufus Perryman, who was known as "Speckled Red."

Black residents of Biddle Street faced obstacles unknown to previous generations. Recreation, welfare, and education centers open to others, barred blacks. The Neighborhood House on North Nineteenth Street was a well-equipped recreational facility, but its staff allowed only whites to walk through its doors. The Catholic Women's League ran a day nursery in the area, but never admitted black children. The playgrounds at Carr Square School remained off limits to blacks until 1941, when the Board of Education made the school itself a segregated black facility.

When St. Louis adopted a "smoke elimination" ordinance in 1940, it worked a further hardship on Biddle Street's residents. The city outlawed cheap smoke-generating coal and mandated a switch to more expensive "smokeless" fuel. On Biddle Street, ninety-one percent of the residents earned less than $100 per month; the new law meant that money that might otherwise have gone to repair property now had to go to buy the approved coal. The added economic burden, together with the historic pattern of flight from declining inner city areas, racial discrimination by landlords and realtors, and the high profits available to slumlords reduced Biddle Street to a sorry state by 1941.

Although Biddle Street still showed signs of life in its bustling crowds and its vendors with their loads of wood, ice, coal, and junk, the street's poverty became more and more evident. More than eighty-five percent of the buildings standing on Biddle Street in 1941 had been constructed between 1860 and 1884, and only one had been constructed since 1914. Residents lived in unpainted houses covered with soot. They had to put rags into holes in the unplastered walls to keep out the cold. Some houses still had dirt floors, and more often than not, residents got their water from a pump in the back yard.

When the federal government made money available for public housing, local authorities jumped at the opportunity to clean up Biddle Street. They launched plans for Carr Square Village, a project designated solely for black residents, to be built along Biddle and Carr streets. Although the project's apartments had too few bedrooms for the large families most in need of shelter, and even though the area was seriously lacking stores, schools, and other services, Carr Square Village enjoyed success from the day it opened its doors in 1942. Unlike the project at the other end of Biddle Street (Pruitt-Igoe), Carr Square Village maintained nearly complete occupancy and proved itself cost-effective over the years. In 1969, Carr Square tenants provided leadership for a citywide rent strike in public housing that won important gains for tenants, not just in St. Louis, but in government-owned housing all across the country. Under tenant management boards the Carr Square and Desoto-Carr projects have continued the long tradition of community solidarity along Biddle Street.

Today's residents are very different from the Carrs, Mullanphys, and Biddles of the 1840s, but they have much in common with the generations of Irish, German, Jewish, and Italian residents of Biddle Street who followed them. Much has changed along those twenty-six blocks over the years, but the people of Biddle Street, in their struggle to build a decent life in the face of great obstacles, remain the same as ever.

The Freidrich Jahn Statue:
The Turnverein Legacy in St. Louis

Friedrich Jahn never lived in St. Louis, and it is highly unlikely that more than a tiny fraction of the local population has even heard of him. But his statue sits in Forest Park as a permanent memorial to his influence on the city. Jahn founded the physical culture movement in Germany in the first part of the nineteenth century, and his ideas shaped the activities of one of St. Louis's most important institutions, the Turnvereins.

The Turnvereins grew out of the experiences and culture of German immigrants in the nineteenth century. Organized as political, gymnastic, and social clubs, the Turnvereins evolved into much more, into a cultural force that continues to influence life in St. Louis. One of many creative adjustments and clever inventions fashioned by immigrants out of their confrontations with the challenges of America, the Turnvereins demonstrate one of the ways in which the seemingly dead past lies embedded in the assumptions and practices of the present.

The original Turnvereins started out in Germany, after Napoleon's successful conquest of 1806. German nationalists bemoaned the fragmentation of their country into numerous ineffectual states, and they longed for a unified nation capable of repelling Napoleon or any future invader. Humiliated by military defeat at the hands of the French, patriotic German reformers resolved to develop their people's strength and character through social clubs devoted to physical culture. Primarily conceived as gymnastic societies and centers of cultural instruction, these clubs also fostered the spread of modern democratic ideals. Their founders believed that centuries of feudalism had left Germany ill-prepared for conflict with the armies of Napoleon, who rode to victory as much on the basis of their egalitarian ideals as on their actual military strengths.

Turnvereins and other physical culture societies played an important role in the development of German liberalism in the nineteenth century. With the failure of the 1848 German Revolution, many liberals migrated to the United States, especially to the "German Triangle" of cities—Cincinnati, Milwaukee, and St. Louis. Immigration exacerbated many existing social problems in these communities, but it also brought an influx of energetic and educated citizens whose ideals and hard work added immeasurably to civic resources.

Members of German Turnvereins came to St. Louis as early as 1839, but they did not establish a local chapter until 1850. Meeting near Lafayette Park on the south side, they soon spread to every neighborhood with a sizable German population. Centers of gymnastic and singing activities at first, the Turnvereins soon took on other functions as well. When the city government tried to ban German picnics by enacting local ordinances prohibiting the consumption of alcoholic beverages out of doors, the Turnvereins constructed meeting houses called Turner Halls to preserve recreations consistent with German traditions.

Like most Germans in St. Louis, the Turners bitterly opposed slavery and supported the abolitionist cause. Missouri Governor Frank Blair mobilized a "home guard," including the Turners, to keep St. Louis loyal to the Union. Blair knew about the Turners' opposition to slavery, but he was also no doubt influenced by their legendary commitment to physical fitness and by the widely-known fact that they kept arsenals inside of the Turner Halls, which added great credibility to their potential as a peace-keeping force.

After the Civil War, Turnvereins experienced their greatest growth. Turner Halls opened at Salisbury and Twentieth Street on the north side, as well as in Tower Grove, Carondelet, Bremen, and other neighborhoods. They presented dances, concerts, gymnastic competitions, and instruction in arts and crafts at these halls, as well as held adult education classes in politics, philosophy, and history. During the General Strike of 1877, strikers held meetings in Turner

Halls, and throughout the last quarter of the nineteenth century, Turners pressured the city to install playgrounds for young people and to institute classes in physical education in the schools.

When the city Board of Education abandoned German language instruction in the public schools in 1888, the Turners initiated Saturday morning German language schools to keep alive their language and culture. Yet increased activity in the Turnvereins at the end of the nineteenth century actually masked a decline in the distinct culture of German-Americans in St. Louis. The cumulative effects of assimilation and discrimination encouraged German-Americans to speak English exclusively, and their very successes in local politics meant that the Turners could rely more on government institutions for educational and recreational opportunities.

At their peak, Turnverein activities involved more than forty thousand members, but World War I marked the beginning of the end for the Turners. Along with many other St. Louisans (and both candidates for president in the 1916 election) the Turnvereins opposed American involvement in World War I. They contended that the war would bring incalculable pain and suffering, but no real peace. Their analysis turned out to be essentially correct, but their German-American heritage became a liability when the United States entered the war and many Americans became caught up in the hysteria of "preparedness." As soon as the United States entered World War I, the St. Louis school system dropped the study of German language and literature from its list of elective courses. The library removed all books by German authors from its shelves. Municipal officials changed German street names like Berlin and Von Verson to Pershing and Enright. Merchants even changed the name of sauerkraut to "liberty cabbage." Under those conditions, a society founded to further German nationalism faced extreme persecution. During the war, the Turnvereins became weaker than ever before, and they would never again be a central force in St. Louis culture.

Organized in the early 1800s as a response to one war, the Turnvereins met their demise in St. Louis in the context of another. But for decades, they carried the banner for physical fitness and intellectual development in the city. They defended St. Louis during the Civil War, and their influence contributed significantly to the establishment of local parks, libraries, playgrounds, and concert halls. They enabled thousands of immigrants to negotiate the confusions of American life, encouraging their assimilation into American culture while preserving their German heritage at the same time.

When explorers, politicians, or soldiers make history, we know exactly what to do. We name streets after them, build statues in their honor, or turn their homes into museums. But only a miniscule portion of the past concerns the activities of people who got their names in newspapers or who left memoirs and records. The history made by common citizens in the course of their everyday lives deserves recognition too. This history often lies beneath the surface appearances of the present, memorialized only in the sedimented layers of culture that influence us in significant if unseen ways. But on Gravois Avenue, on Salisbury Street, and throughout the city, you can still see buildings that once housed Turner Halls, and in Forest Park, you can see the statue of Friedrich Jahn, which serves as an appropriate and justified reminder of their influence and importance.

The Soccer Fields of St. Louis: Ethnic Identity and the "Big Game"

Many cities enjoy "big games" between local rivals. These are usually football contests between squads of imported gladiators who just happen to be wearing the colors of their respective schools. In St. Louis, the "big game" matches the soccer squads from St. Louis University and Southern Illinois University at Edwardsville, who compete for a trophy called the "Bronze Boot" and for some distinctly local bragging rights.

For more than a century, soccer has been St. Louis's game. Local players fill the rosters of professional teams throughout the country, and one small block in south St. Louis alone (the 5400 block of Daggett Avenue) has produced six professional soccer players. Over the years, rivalries between schools, neighborhoods, and ethnic groups traditionally have been decided on the soccer field.

Soccer came to St. Louis as a consequence of working-class migration from Europe in the nineteenth century. German brewery workers, Italian terra-cotta craftsmen, Scottish railroad employees, and Irish factory hands had little in common beyond the alienations of labor, but soccer provided them with a common activity. Industrial, ethnic, neighborhood, and church teams built solidarity within groups and allowed for (mostly) friendly rivalries against others.

Corporations including Scullin Steel and St. Louis Screw sponsored soccer teams in the nineteenth century to provide their workers with recreation and a chance to vent the frustrations of the work week. Ethnic benevolent societies and fraternal orders like the Scottish Thistles and the Irish Hibernians fielded teams as part of their social activities and perhaps as a means of settling ethnic rivalries by some means other than fistfights. Working-class neighborhoods coalesced around soccer teams as well. The Kensingtons took their name from the north side street that provided the main thoroughfare in their neighborhood. They won every game they played during the 1889–1890 season without surrendering even a single goal, and their success served as a focal point of community pride for years.

Close ties between the game of soccer and other aspects of ethnic working-class life made the games more than just diversions. Irish teams played benefit games to help raise money for the defense of the Irish patriot, Patrick O'Donnell, while he was on trial for his life on charges of having murdered a police informant. Teams in the mostly German and Irish Sodality Football League frequently donated the gate receipts from their games to the families of police officers and fire fighters injured in the line of duty. Soccer fields themselves went beyond service as the site of athletic contests; at Seventeenth and Jefferson in Kerry Patch, at Jefferson and Cass in midtown, and at Compton and the railroad tracks on the south side, soccer fields became multipurpose centers of social life for immigrants and their families.

The history of local soccer teams provides a useful index to the assimilation of St. Louis ethnic groups. In the early years of the twentieth century, the "German Sport Club" made its mark featuring the continental style of soccer in the Municipal League in Carondelet Park. They departed radically from the British style that had dominated the game locally ever since the Blue Bells, a team made up of Scottish railroad workers, had won repeated championships in the 1890s. But by 1933, most of the players on the "German Sport Club" had Irish names and played the British style. In contrast, the Italian and Spanish teams retained their distinct identities and styles until well after World War II.

In the years when most of the Italian population of St. Louis lived in "Little Italy" near Columbus Square at Tenth and Carr streets downtown, they made little impact on local soccer. But when large numbers of Italians began settling on the Hill near Macklind and Southwest Avenues, they formed their own teams and enjoyed extraordinary success. On the Hill, soccer actually enjoyed more popularity among the children and grandchildren of immigrants than it did among the first generation, as teams from that neighborhood played an increasingly prominent role in the sport as the years went by. By the late 1920s, a team sponsored by the Calcaterra Undertakers relied exclusively on the talents of Italian players from the Hill. In 1931, Father John Wieberg organized the first team from St. Ambrose Parish, and Hill teams captured local and national championships throughout the 1930s and 1940s. During championship games at Sportsman's Park on Grand and Dodier, hostile fans sometimes yelled "send those foreigners back to Italy" at the Hill players, even though almost all of them had been born in St. Louis.

Soccer teams representing the Spanish and Mexican communities became important as early as the 1920s. Drawn to the area by opportunities for employment in the local zinc and smelting industries, these groups lived near the American Zinc works in Fairmont City, Illinois on the East Side and along South Broadway near the Edgar Zinc Plant. Teams from "Spanish Town"—the blocks from 6900 to 7300 South Broadway—represented Our Lady of Cordova Church and the Asturias Club. In 1949, the Spanish-American Club, managed by Manuel Fernandez, won the Municipal League championship.

The enduring popularity of soccer in St. Louis testifies to the power of the city's immigrant past. Some labor historians estimate that as much as eighty percent of the American factory workforce in America in the nineteenth century consisted of foreign-born laborers, and population figures in St. Louis seem to support that judgment. Of the 350,518 St. Louis residents in 1880, nearly two-thirds were either first- or second-generation immigrants. In 1900, 111,356 St. Louisans had been born outside the country and an additional 239,170 had foreign-born parents. In a city with a total population of 575,238, this meant that immigrants or their children accounted for more than sixty percent of the total.

Legal restrictions on immigration in the 1920s and the dispersal of working-class families into the suburbs after World War II seriously disrupted local soccer activities. The Municipal League had 119 teams in 1947, but had disbanded completely by 1957. Yet youth teams sponsored by local businesses (notably the Kutis Funeral Home) gained national prominence in the 1950s and 1960s, while St. Louis University dominated the NCAA soccer tournament in the 1960s. The 1970s witnessed an increase in soccer competition for young people all across the country, and not surprisingly, St. Louis played an important part in that revival. The Bronze Boot game and the high visibility garnered by St. Louis players throughout college and professional soccer testify to the endurance of local traditions. Soccer in other cities may be just another sport, but in St. Louis it is more than a game, it is a living reminder of a precious collective heritage.

Polish Falcons Hall:
Social Welfare and Self-Help

For more than eighty years, the Polish Falcons lodge has been an important part of community life on the north side of St. Louis. Founded in 1905 as a gymnastics club and mutual aid society, the organization continues to serve the Polish-American community with a variety of cultural and athletic activities from its building on the north side at 2013 St. Louis Avenue. But the significance of this lodge, and others like it, goes beyond the immediate services it renders to its own members. Fraternal organizations and lodge halls have responded to the needs of ethnic groups in ways that have had lasting effects on the quality of urban life, providing benefits to a broader community than their own memberships.

At the turn of the century, the streets of St. Louis teemed with refugees from all over the world. Immigrants from Poland, Greece, Germany, Ireland, Russia, Italy, and the American South lived in the crowded row houses and apartment buildings lining the streets closest to the Mississippi River. Peddlers of all nationalities sold coal, wood, or ice from dilapidated carts in the streets, while small bakeries and delicatessens specialized in "exotic" cuisines that kept alive memories (and tastes and smells) of the lands that the immigrants had left behind.

Manufacturing and transportation industries profiting from cheap immigrant labor tended to both unite and divide the newcomers. On the one hand, life in the factory or urban neighborhood gave immigrants from diverse backgrounds a common experience. Without capital or marketable skills, most of them worked long hours under debilitating conditions, striving to earn enough money to pay rent for meager apartments vacated by previous generations of immigrants. On the other hand, employers and politicians encouraged ethnic divisions, playing one group against another in order to lessen their leverage as a whole. Oppressed by class, but divided by language, religion, and customs, urban immigrants turned potential liabilities into assets by exaggerating their ethnic identities, forming ties of solidarity on the basis of nationality.

Thus ethnic identity in America stemmed in part from class strategies for advancement. Ethnic appeals produced an effective solidarity and an affective unity too often missing from appeals to classwide unity. The existence of ethnic neighborhoods provided business opportunities to service the special needs of those communities which escaped the notice of wealthier, less sensitive entrepreneurs from the outside. Most important, ethnic solidarity could provide mutual aid and services unavailable by other means.

For example, individual immigrants often lacked the resources for burial insurance, but cooperative efforts by ethnic lodges could guarantee a decent burial and funeral for a loved one. Workers facing the risks of disability or unemployment in a time before government-sponsored Social Security or unemployment compensation could look to their ethnic lodges for some measure of help in an emergency. Perhaps most important, in an era when factory time replaced the farming day, and when paved city streets took the place of rural fields, fraternal orders could provide opportunities for sports, self-improvement and socializing with others.

Groups like the German Turnvereins and the Polish Falcons provided otherwise unavailable gymnastic opportunities for St. Louis residents. Elite citizens sometimes donated land to the city for public parks, but usually these had no playground equipment or sports fields. Some, like Carr Square Park, even had rules stipulating that pedestrians remain on the sidewalks and keep off the grass. Under those circumstances, a lodge hall with a fully equipped gymnasium could be a precious resource for working-class immigrants and their families.

The Polish Falcons originated in Poland as the *Sokol Polski* in 1867. They came to the United States ten years later, with the founding of Polish Falcon Nest #1 in Chicago. Victor Imbierowicz, Stan Lewandowski, and Gabriel Jeglerski formed the St. Louis chapter for men, Nest #45, in 1905. Marie Mielcarek established Nest #104 for women in St. Louis in 1908. The Falcons held gymnastics classes at Stolle's Hall on Thirteenth and Biddle streets (where a few years earlier "Frankie" had shot "Johnnie" in a lover's spat that inspired the popular song), and later moved to their own hall in the 1900 block of Cass Avenue. In 1919, Nest #45 incorporated with Nest #104 into one organization with both male and female members. In the early 1930s, the lodge moved to its present building on St. Louis Avenue.

Near the Polish-American St. Stanislaus Church close to what used to be Kerry Patch, one of the city's most famous Irish-American neighborhoods, the Polish Falcons Hall provides an important link to the past as well as an interesting manifestation of that past in the present. Many Polish-Americans moved out of the neighborhood and into North County in the years following World War II, but the organization remained headquartered in the hall on St. Louis Avenue. Built by local brewer Charles Stifel in the 1880s, the building's history embodies an important part of the Polish Falcons organization. The Falcons not only managed to purchase it during the Depression of the 1930s, but a coordinated community effort salvaged it for the group in 1934 when it appeared as if they might have to default on their mortgage. Remaining on St. Louis Avenue reminds them of the struggles that they went through to obtain ownership of the building, and at the same time serves as a commitment to the future of the city that has served the needs of succeeding waves of immigrants in Kerry Patch since the nineteenth century.

Today, the three hundred and twenty-five members of the Polish Falcons continue to enjoy gymnastics, folk dancing, and other social activities in the big hall on St. Louis Avenue. Yet the political victories won over the years by working people in this country make ethnic mutual aid societies and their recreational facilities less important than before. Combined political action by immigrants and their descendants helped win public commitments to playgrounds, playing fields, old-age pensions, unemployment compensation, federally financed mortgage loans, and other programs that were all once the sole domain of ethnic fraternal organizations. By demonstrating the benefits of mutual aid, the fraternal lodges of the nineteenth century helped create the demand for policies providing public services and amenities that have benefited subsequent generations. The incorporation of their agenda into public policy has hardly exhausted the possibilities of fraternal lodges. In recent years they have become even more important because of their role in perpetuating ethnic pride and demonstrating the importance of ethnic diversity in St. Louis's past and present.

It is sad but true that the same culture that so reluctantly assimilated immigrants and their families into the economic benefits of American abundance also proved ruthless in attempting to beat down their ethnic cultural heritages and to reconstruct them as a formless mass of consumers. From discrimination in employment to outright cultural ridicule, immigrants faced terrible pressures to give up their unique and precious ethnic legacies. Organizations like the Polish Falcons keep alive memories of their specific legacy, but they also remind us that the achievements of America have been the sum total of contributions by people from varied cultures and backgrounds. One need not romanticize the ethnic heritage of St. Louis to cherish it. In the shared collective memory of groups like the Polish Falcons lies a precious and humane tradition that guided the actions of people in the past, and which continues to inform and shape the best parts of our culture today.

Meramec Highlands: Where St. Louis Learned to Play

A taste of cotton candy, a ride on a roller coaster, or a glimpse of a Ferris wheel can evoke sensations and feelings that tug at the heart in particularly compelling ways. Whether St. Louisans recall Six Flags Over Mid-America, Forest Park Highlands, or even the Pike at the 1904 World's Fair, amusement parks have a special power to bring back the feelings of childhood as a time when the world was waiting to be discovered.

Yet amusement parks are a fairly recent invention, and their origins had nothing to do with nostalgia for childhood. St. Louis's first amusement park, Meramec Highlands in Kirkwood, catered mainly to adults, and concerned itself more with pleasure in the present than with memories of the past. More than a mere playground or business venture, it played a crucial role in changing attitudes about work and play in St. Louis. In fact, it is no exaggeration to say that turn-of-the-century St. Louisans developed part of the vital psychic resources necessary for life in the modern world in this amusement park.

Meramec Highlands opened its doors in May 1895 as a complete 438-acre resort, boasting a hotel, health spa, swimming area, and amusement park. Rail and streetcar lines brought waves of visitors to enjoy such attractions as a steam-powered merry-go-round, boating, horseback riding, and dancing. Of course these were not new activities for St. Louisans; in one form or another they had all been around for years. The novelty of Meramec Highlands came in its use of space as an enclosed area totally dedicated to commercial leisure-time activities. The amusement park emerged as a kind of liberated zone, a place reserved exclusively for pleasure, excitement, and risk.

The attractions and sensations offered at Meramec Highlands differed sharply from life in the rest of the city. Victorian values emphasizing hard work, thrift, abstinence, discipline and propriety still held sway in America in the 1890s. Rigid codes regulated social behavior; men could tip their hats to women only under certain conditions, and ladies never initiated conversations with strange gentlemen. Photographs of crowds from that era depict strangers passing each other carefully and walking purposefully to their destinations. The world of work held first claim on individuals, and any vices that might privilege pleasure over duty came to be seen as a threat to hearth and home.

Victorian values worked effectively to help American farmers and immigrants from rural backgrounds make the adjustment to the demands of an industrializing society in the years after the Civil War. But this repression of pleasure and its displacement of desire became something of an anachronism by the 1890s when the diligent labors of Victorian workers produced more commodities than thrifty consumers would buy. The material surpluses made possible by industrial labor needed consumers motivated by ostentation, display, and materialism, not frugality and repression.

Amusement parks like Meramec Highlands responded to that crisis by providing safe havens for experimenting with new values. People at these parks could act out desires prohibited in everyday life but acceptable as play. Stimulated by the popularity of the Midway at the 1894 Chicago World's Fair and by the growth of streetcar lines connecting central cities with inexpensive suburban property, amusement parks like New York's Coney Island and St. Louis's Meramec Highlands captured the public fancy in the 1890s.

In an age that doted on passive spectator sports and frowned on excessive physical exertion, the amusement park created a space for active recreation. Instead of watching a horse race, baseball game, or boxing match, visitors to Meramec Highlands could ride horses and pedal bicycles, row boats, or swim in the Meramec River. Crowds lingered and strolled in scenic areas, as good-natured banter replaced the solemn reserve that characterized public interactions on Victorian streets.

It was not just that crowds flocked around the attractions at Meramec Highlands. The crowds themselves became an attraction. Young men and women might be prohibited from conversing openly (or meeting secretly) in their neighborhoods, but they could have "privacy in public" at Meramec Highlands. Forbidden behavior became acceptable amidst the crowds and revelry at the amusement park.

Five hundred passengers a day took the Frisco Railroad trains from Union Station in downtown St. Louis out to Meramec Highlands. The line ran nine trains each way on weekdays, and four trains on Sundays. The Highlands Inn hosted as many as 125 guests at a time in its luxurious accommodations spread over five stories. The park rented conservative "bathing costumes" to guests to preserve a certain standard of propriety, but mixed bathing among strangers by itself amounted to a sharp break with Victorian conventions.

Meramec Highlands closed in 1910, victimized by poor management, undercapitalization, and vandalism. But it did its work well in its brief history. St. Louisans liked the new forms of social interaction and the new definitions of public space explored at the park, and they incorporated those values into the rest of their lives. Play became a legitimate social activity. When commodities like motion pictures and phonograph records became available, St. Louisans were ready to buy them. The loosening of Victorian codes helped shape the psychic resources necessary for a modern economy based on the sale of consumer goods with their emphases on fashion, luxury, and immediate gratification.

Yet while these changes have eased the flow of consumer goods into our lives, they have not done very much to make everyday life more playful or social. Today we encounter no value crisis at an amusement park; indeed, its activities and design all too perfectly reflect those of the shopping mall and the appliance-filled suburban home. Nor do we realize anything new about the potential uses of social space at the amusement park today. We may marvel at mechanical tricks and introduce our children to a world of commercialized leisure, but although we have learned to spend our money and to cultivate our desires for commodities, we have yet to bring back into urban life the kinds of active social spaces that St. Louisans got a glimpse of in the 1890s at Meramec Highlands.

University City:
The Suburb Created by a Con Man

University City has long enjoyed a well-deserved reputation as one of the most pleasant and attractive communities in the St. Louis area. From the majestic sculpted lions overlooking the entrance to the University Heights subdivision to the startling tower that houses the municipal government offices, a unique and distinctive vision lies behind the physical grace of the city. Judging by appearances alone, this suburb on the western border of the St. Louis city limits represents a triumph of turn-of-the-century urban planning.

Yet the guiding genius behind University City had no credentials as an architect or a city planner. In fact, Edward Gardner Lewis's preeminent talent seemed to rest in staying out of jail and avoiding the consequences of his many acts of swindling and fraud. The man who founded University City and who served as its first mayor started his career in Connecticut peddling "cures" for tobacco cravings. He initially came to the Midwest as a salesman for pesticides that he promised (fraudulently) would kill mosquitoes and cockroaches, and he left St. Louis in a hurry, barely a step ahead of postal authorities and his many creditors. Somehow, in the midst of all this chicanery and guile, Lewis found the time to design and implement his plans for University City. In 1906, Lewis incorporated University City and became its first mayor.

Typical of the legendary, upwardly mobile entrepreneurs of his era, Lewis started out with nothing and wound up a millionaire. Unfortunately, he did so by relieving gullible customers of their lives' savings, promising them a stake in his growing empire as a certain path toward easy wealth. Born in Hartford, Connecticut in 1868, Lewis dropped out of college to seek his fortune selling dry goods and watches. He came to St. Louis in 1895 and made money selling mosquito repellent, patent medicines, and candy. Profits from these ventures went into newer and ever more elaborate schemes. In 1899, Lewis entered the publishing business with his first magazine, the *Winner,* featuring pages of advertisements for another Lewis enterprise—the Progressive Watch Company. He promised his readers financial happiness if they would only purchase from him the right to sell Progressive Watches to their friends. Postal fraud inspectors charged Lewis with running an illegal "pyramid" scheme with his watches, initiating a twenty-year battle between the government and the publisher. But trouble with the law only induced Lewis to redouble his money-making efforts in other spheres.

Lewis's flamboyant business practices and his brazen advertising claims hardly set him apart from most businessmen of his day. Between 1890 and 1920, traditions of Victorian repression and restraint in America gave way to a new consumer ethic. Advertising played a pivotal role in transforming thrifty, sober, and industrious Victorians into free-spending uninhibited consumers. Exaggerated claims typified the advertising of the day, which aimed to sell an entire lifestyle, not just individual products. In an unregulated market, before the advent of the Federal Trade Commission and the Pure Food and Drug Administration, fraudulent practices abounded, and nearly every advertiser promised miraculous results from consumer purchases. Businessmen like Lewis sold "the sizzle" instead of the steak, constantly stoking the fires of desire in consumers in order to set them up for the next sale.

In 1902, Lewis transformed the *Winner* into the *Woman's Magazine* and moved his publishing operations from downtown St. Louis to what is now University City. Lewis patterned the *Woman's Magazine* after the *Ladies Home Journal,* speaking to women as a specialized constituency and market. He mixed a mild feminism with sophisticated marketing campaigns aimed at female consumers. Always fascinated by new technology, Lewis invested wisely in new printing equipment and in modern methods of distribution. Soon the *Woman's Magazine* claimed 1.6 million readers.

Advertisements in his magazine reflected Lewis's many financial interests. He sold residential lots in University Heights, established a "People's Bank," and invited readers to join his American Woman's League, an organization whose major activity seemed to be selling new memberships in itself. Highly questionable financial practices lay behind each of these endeavors, and in 1905, the U.S. Postal Service launched a vindictive all-out attack on Lewis. Postal authorities returned all mail sent to him (some three thousand to twenty-two thousand pieces per day) back to the original correspondents with the word "fraudulent" stamped in red on it, costing the magazine thousands of subscriptions. Complicated stock transfers among his many enterprises brought Lewis into federal court in 1912, but a jury refused to convict him. Legal defense costs and the diminishing reputation of his businesses undermined many of Lewis's ventures. Later that year, he left St. Louis to take up a career selling stock in abandoned mines and dried-up oil wells to gullible investors.

Lewis's enterprises enjoyed enormous popularity because they offered millions of people a glimpse of the good life. He combined the instincts of a socialist with the motives of a capitalist, generating an intense loyalty among his customers. Lewis once proposed a National Woman's Exchange designed to find national markets for women interested in selling crafts and art work. At a time when a majority of Americans did not finish high school, Lewis's "People's

University" enrolled fifty thousand mail-order students eager to learn practical skills like stenography, law, and nursing, as well as traditional academic subjects including languages, composition, and art from Lewis's surprisingly reputable and competent faculty. A mail-order lending library provided books for readers unable to obtain them by other means. In these projects, Lewis tapped into the long traditions of self-improvement and self-help in American culture, offering services similar to those provided by the farmers' Grange association or ethnic mutual aid societies in an earlier day, and by government in later years. Operating during a time of transition, when cooperatives increasingly failed and when government had not yet taken on many social welfare functions, Lewis gave his investors and customers a rare outlet for their economic, cultural, and educational aspirations.

University City became the focal point of Lewis's empire. It remains today a testament to the socially responsible side of his imagination. Lewis spared no expense designing and implementing his vision of suburban life as an enclave free from the pollution and overcrowding of the industrial city. His landscaped streets and public parks anticipated the "greenbelt" idea used in subsequent suburbs, and distinctive touches of style and design alerted present and future residents to the community's unique character. Lewis commissioned the sculptor George Julian Zolnay to create the lion statues overlooking Delmar Boulevard. He financed the Italian Renaissance-styled city hall, and he patterned his printing plant after one of the great temples of Egypt.

After leaving the area in 1912, Lewis resumed his entrepreneurial career with tragic results. He declared bankruptcy in 1924, and four years later began serving a prison sentence for mail fraud. He died in 1950, penniless and all but unrecognized for the vision which brought so much excitement to turn-of-the-century St. Louis.

The strange career of Edward Gardner Lewis reminds us that history is made by both saints and sinners, and that it sometimes takes an eccentric to impose a bold vision on the commonplace realities of everyday life. University City was not founded by a saint, but it owes a lot to the positive social vision and fearless bravado of its all-too-human founder. As Susan Waugh McDonald points out, "Although he left many creditors poorer, Lewis certainly left University City richer for all his imagination and enterprise." In life, no less than in mechanics, sometimes it takes a good crank to get things started.

Homer G. Phillips Hospital: Promises to Keep

When city officials finally closed Homer G. Phillips Hospital as a full-service health-care facility in 1979, they viewed their decision as regrettable, but necessary. The city could not afford two hospitals, and outside consultants and medical authorities agreed that City Hospital could provide better service to more of the public. Although these officials anticipated an immediate negative response from some quarters, they hoped that the long-range logic of their position would prevail over short-term emotional opposition.

They were wrong. From the start, the decision to close Phillips Hospital provoked anger and action from black St. Louisans. Demonstrators risked winter cold and summer heat to keep their cause before the public. Supporters of the hospital erected barricades to prevent the police from closing it, and more than one hundred people were arrested in the many protests that brought back into the streets such veteran leaders of civil rights protest in St. Louis as Percy Green, Dick Gregory, and Ivory Perry.

Mayor James Conway was voted out of office largely because of his sponsorship of the shutdown of Homer G. Phillips, and a citywide referendum in 1981 demonstrated that sixty percent of the voters wanted to keep the hospital open. But despite newly elected Mayor Vincent Schoemehl's promises to keep it operative as a full-time city hospital, the doors on Whittier Street were eventually locked for good in 1984.

What accounts for the depth of feeling about Phillips? Why would the black community rally around an antiquated facility that would cost millions of dollars to reopen? Why would they ignore the experts who said that better health care could be delivered at City Hospital? The answer is only partly a matter of health care or economics; in essence, the fight over Phillips was a fight about history. More than any other issue, the closing of Homer G. Phillips revealed that black people and white people in St. Louis do not share the same understanding of the past, and as a result, they have differing perceptions about the present and the future.

It took a sustained protest movement to create Phillips Hospital in the first place. Leaders of the black community had urged the city to establish a full-service health care facility on the north side as early as 1915. They pointed to the need for a teaching hospital for training black doctors, and they complained bitterly about the poor-quality health care available to blacks at the poorly funded and segregated City Hospital #2. These requests fell on deaf ears until 1923 when Mayor Henry Kiel needed black support for a comprehensive bond issue aimed at repairing the city's deteriorating infrastructure. Kiel negotiated an agreement with black attorney and community leader Homer G. Phillips: if blacks supported the bond issue, $1 million of the $87 million would go for a hospital to serve their needs.

Blacks voted for the bond issue by a margin of better than four to one, although it proved so popular among white voters that black votes did not prove decisive. Because of the bond issue, St. Louis built Kiel Auditorium, Soldiers Memorial, and Aloe Plaza. The city used the money raised by it to make major improvements in streets, sewers, and other municipal services. But city officials contended that they had no obligation to build a hospital *in* the black community; instead they proposed to spend the $1 million on a "colored extension" of City Hospital under the supervision of white administrators. For years the city tried to back out of its commitment, and it was not until 1932, one year after the death of Homer G. Phillips, that construction started on the hospital that would eventually bear his name.

Reneging on the promise to build a teaching and health-care hospital for blacks represented just one of many obstacles that white St. Louis placed in the path of black progress. Private employers paid lower wages to black workers, and during hard times designated them as the first to be fired. Government statistics revealed that eighty percent of the black workforce was either unemployed or underemployed in 1933. Labor unions like that of the railway clerks banned blacks from membership entirely, while others confined them to low-paying job classifications or placed them in segregated locals under white domination. The Urban League's Federated Block Units had to wage repeated campaigns to get the city to extend routine services to black neighborhoods and to get federal relief funds dispersed to blacks as well as to whites.

Racial discrimination so pervaded business in St. Louis that even when the city consented to build Homer G. Phillips Hospital it allowed no blacks to get skilled jobs building it. As with the construction of schools, even those in black neighborhoods, the city insisted it could find no blacks qualified to do the work—a flimsy excuse but an underhanded way of reinforcing the discriminatory practices of construction unions. City officials refused applications for work on Phillips by twenty black plasterers, thirty-one black carpenters, thirty-five black electricians, and forty-four black painters, all of whom either had union cards from other cities or who had done comparable work in St. Louis.

Yet unceasing struggle brought victory. On February 22, 1937, Homer G. Phillips Hospital opened its doors as a full-service health-care facility. It immediately took on both local and national importance. The hospital complemented Sumner High School and Poro Beauty College as major employers and educational institutions in black St. Louis. Nationally, it became a major center for the education and training of black health-care professionals. Just as black north side residents knew that Sumner High School and Poro College really served national constituencies (how many black communities had a first-class high school or a business that could teach employable skills?), they understood that Homer G. Phillips Hospital was a precious resource for the health and welfare of all black Americans.

Despite inadequate funding, callous disregard from the white medical establishment, and shameful neglect from the major medical schools, Homer G. Phillips functioned as a first-rate hospital. Its decline in the 1970s came not from internal causes, but from the effects of local and national forces and their impact upon north St. Louis.

Urban renewal moved thousands of people out of the Mill Creek Valley into north side neighborhoods in the 1960s. Federal Housing Agency loan practices favored construction of new suburbs over renovation of older neighborhoods. With more poor people crowding into poorer housing, and with suburbanization draining the city of its tax base, hospitals and health-care institutions moved westward, those institutions left behind became resources of last resort, primarily used by the indigent.

By 1965, rumors began to circulate about the closing of Homer G. Phillips. Black voters that year cast their ballots for A. J. Cervantes in the mayoral primary election, because they believed (rightly or wrongly) that Raymond Tucker intended to close the hospital. Cervantes and every subsequent mayor dropped hints about closing the hospital, but it was not until the Conway and Schoemehl administrations that final actions were taken.

During their protests against the closing of the north side hospital, black St. Louis knew all about the highways that went right by City Hospital compared with the narrow streets around Phillips. They knew all about the estimated costs of restoring Phillips to service as a full medical facility. They knew about the medical schools, financial experts, and hospital administrators who argued that City Hospital would be easier to salvage. But they knew about other things as well.

They knew about John Berry Meachum who, before the Civil War, had run a school on a boat in the middle of the Mississippi River so that blacks could get an education, even though the state of Missouri made it illegal for them to do so. They knew about Charlton Tandy and his relentless fights to get blacks employed as teachers and postal workers, and his long struggle against overwhelming odds to integrate St. Louis streetcars. They knew that nothing has been given to the black community without a struggle, and that promises made can be promises broken. Assurances about the future have always been plentiful; viable institutions serving the black community have been few.

They knew what all of us in St. Louis should know. A people, its history, and its institutions are not to be trifled with. Justice, like freedom in Thomas Jefferson's admonition, can only be secured through eternal vigilance.

People

Chris von der Ahe:
Beer and Baseball in Urban Life

To the average fan, the importance of baseball in St. Louis probably revolves around memories of people like Rogers Hornsby, Stan Musial, and Bob Gibson with their heroic exploits on the diamond. But baseball has been important to St. Louis off the field as well, as a business enterprise, as a symbol of civic pride, and as a battleground for competing cultural norms.

St. Louis's first great championship team, the St. Louis Browns of the 1880s, had an enormous impact on urban life. Their eccentric owner, Chris von der Ahe, typified one species of nineteenth-century businessman, and his many battles with players and fans encapsulated many of the social tensions facing an industrializing America. Von der Ahe's gift for promotion helped stimulate new patterns of leisure, and his masterful ability to grasp the connection between sports and commerce helped him to reshape not only urban neighborhoods but the values of their inhabitants as well.

A German immigrant, von der Ahe owned a small store selling beer and groceries near Spring and Sullivan streets on the city's near north side. Al Spink, a local newspaperman whose family started the *Sporting News,* approached von der Ahe with the suggestion that he sponsor a baseball team. In words that would prove prophetic, von der Ahe replied that he knew nothing about the game, but "if it sells beer, then I'm all for it."

It did. The Browns' owner sold his beverages at the games and used his prominence as the team's owner to publicize his other ventures, like the residential apartments named after star players that he constructed near the ballfield. Ever mindful of the beer business, he put saloons on the corner of every north side block that he built. He even convinced one of the local streetcar lines to invest in the team, arguing that a more competitive team would draw residents to the neighborhood who would use the streetcars everyday as well as stimulating traffic on the line during game days.

Despite their owner's legendary frugality when it came to paying salaries, the Browns won the American Association championship every year between 1885 and 1888—largely on the strength of talented players, including the skilled Jack Glasscock, the speedy but vicious Arlie Latham, and the memorably named "Ice Box" Chamberlain. Off the field, the team's owner certainly knew how to promote his business. During one World Series, he kept his players at a local hotel and had them transported to the ballpark in open, horse-drawn carriages. When amusement parks became popular in the 1890s, von der Ahe turned the Browns' ballfield into the "Coney Island of the West" complete with a merry-go-round, beer garden, shoot-the-chute ride, and fireworks. He hired an all-female band to entertain before games, and even placed a race track around the field.

The Browns' owner tried to give people a reason to attend games even if they did not like baseball. His advertisements in foreign language ethnic newspapers presented baseball as an American institution to assimilation-hungry immigrants. At the same time he stressed the "natural" splendor of the field as an antidote to the overcrowding and pollution of the industrial city. Von der Ahe even devised special seating arrangements and discount tickets for female fans when he noticed their attraction to the handsome first baseman and player-manager Charlie Comiskey.

Unfortunately, he never learned much about the game itself. Once, von der Ahe thought it a good idea to order his players to not hit the ball to the other team's fielders. Whenever the other team got a hit, he complained that his fielders were out of position. He once boasted that he owned the "biggest diamond" in the league until Comiskey informed him that all baseball diamonds had to be the same size. "Well," snapped von der Ahe, "then I've got the biggest infield."

The success of the Browns gave von der Ahe an economic and social status that would have been denied him by other means. He found his success all that much more gratifying because the socially prominent Lucas family had experienced mixed results from their baseball ventures—the St. Louis Red Stockings and the St. Louis Maroons. By catering to neglected and misunderstood markets, and by creating markets where none had previously existed, von der Ahe found an unexpected route to respectability. The city's name and reputation became connected to von der Ahe's private business, and he found in this way that his profit-making enterprise enjoyed the status of a civic resource.

In addition, the "moral lessons" of baseball appealed to upwardly mobile capitalists like von der Ahe in the nineteenth century. Traditional festivals and carnivals tended to unite people, but professional competition clearly separated winners from losers, participants from spectators, and owners from players. The "win at all costs" mentality displayed on the baseball field reinforced the "survival of the fittest" ethic dominant in business. For example, one year after the Browns lost a playoff series to Detroit, von der Ahe punished the players for losing by keeping all of the gate receipts from the games for himself. Baseball was one enterprise where workers had no rights, not even the right to quit work and find a job with another team. Club owners could play out power fantasies in the sports business that exceeded even the already reactionary standards prevalent in the nineteenth-century business world. For instance, Cap Anson, owner of the Chicago White Sox succeeded in barring black players from professional ball in 1876, even though more than thirty had played before that without provoking any trouble from fans or other players. However ungrounded, Anson's preferences remained the official policy of major league baseball until 1947.

Baseball offered rewards for nineteenth-century fans as well, although of course to a lesser degree than for the owners. A day at the ballpark could offer escape from the demands of the world of work. To people raised in a Victorian culture stressing hard work, thrift, discipline, and repression, a day at the ballpark provided a welcome dose of hedonism. Ethnic heroes like the Irish and German players who dominated the game in the 1870s (like the Czechs, Jews, Italians, and Poles who came later) offered the hope of assimilation and upward mobility to their fans with their much publicized performances on the field. For residents of an industrial city, the ballfield offered a nostalgic glimpse of nature, a chance to spend an afternoon on a grass field enjoying the sun, with no machinery to be seen. Baseball's rhythms predated industrial time, as well. Instead of a clock, each side got an equal number of turns at bat. Just as owners like Chris von der Ahe used baseball to play out their fantasies of labor/management relations, fans could use the game to revive memories of a time when work and play were not so rigidly divided.

A baseball team might also serve as a locus of civic pride in ways not intended by the team owner. Local residents felt deeply wounded when New York Giants manager John McGraw suggested that the intense summer heat in St. Louis guaranteed that no St. Louis team would ever win a world championship. When the 1926 Cardinals defeated the New York Yankees to win the city's first championship of the modern (after 1900) era, many St. Louisans and fans throughout the South and the West treated the team's triumph as a populist victory over Eastern plutocracy.

In the long run, Chris von der Ahe's penny-pinching proved counterproductive, and his ignorance about baseball outstripped his promotional genius and luck. He lost control of his team and spent his last years in poverty and anonymity. But professional baseball permanently transformed the city of St. Louis. The neighborhoods developed by Chris von der Ahe still bear the marks of his enterprise and imagination. Generations of local residents have bonded together in mutual agony and ecstasy as their teams' fortunes have waxed and waned.

Chris von der Ahe proved that professional baseball could bring money into the coffers of local merchants, that it could shape the face of urban development, and that it could stimulate the sale of beer. He did not live to see the full flowering of these possibilities, but others who have followed in his footsteps seem to have learned quite well from his example.

Kate Chopin: The Awakening

From all outward appearances, nothing out of the ordinary seemed to be taking place in the big house at 3317 Morgan Street in St. Louis in the 1890s. An attractive widow in her forties, a member of one of the most respected families in the city, lived in that house. Little in her daily routine distinguished her from her neighbors. On bright, brisk days she liked to walk along Olive or Washington streets to look into the shop windows and collect her thoughts. Then she would stroll home, settle into the Morris chair by the window (so she could see the trees and the sky) and pick up a pen and start to write. There she produced one of the great masterpieces of American literature, a novel titled *The Awakening*.

In her career as a writer, Kate Chopin made major contributions to the intellectual and cultural life of St. Louis. Her literary accomplishments secured her significant recognition and reward. Yet her honest portrayal of a married woman's sexual restlessness in *The Awakening* brought condemnation from many quarters. Moralists derided the book as degenerate and morbid. One St. Louis critic suggested that the label "poison" be affixed to it. Old friends expelled Chopin from membership in private clubs. Devastated by the vehement hostility provoked by her novel, Chopin wrote little else before her death in 1904. She died thinking of her work as a failure. But modern readers have rediscovered *The Awakening* and have celebrated it as a work of genius ahead of its time.

Born Kate O'Flaherty in St. Louis in 1850, she attended the St.

Louis Academy of the Sacred Heart and received a fine Catholic education. Thomas O'Flaherty, her father, left his native Ireland as a young man to come to St. Louis, where he made a substantial fortune in business. He married Eliza Farris from one of the old Creole families that originally moved to St. Louis from New Orleans in the early days of European settlement, and the couple lived in a fashionable house on Eighth Street between Chouteau and Gratiot. Kate O'Flaherty grew up listening to tales of old St. Louis told by her maternal grandmother. She spoke both French and English at home at the insistence of her parents, who wanted her to be aware of both sides of her heritage.

Two tragedies marred an otherwise happy childhood. Her father died in 1855 when a railroad bridge across the Gasconade River collapsed and killed O'Flaherty and twenty-four other train passengers. He had been one of the founders of the Pacific Railroad, and the accident occurred on the line's inaugural run between St. Louis and Jefferson City. What started as a day of celebration for the railroad's executives ended as a day of horror.

Five years later, the Civil War divided the nation and the city of St. Louis into warring factions. Motivated by loyalty to French-speaking Louisiana, and convinced that slavery was actually a benign system, young Kate's family sided with the South and mourned the loss of loved ones who fought for the Confederacy.

Yet once the war ended, the O'Flaherty family resumed its comfortable position in St. Louis society. Kate attracted considerable attention from young men fascinated by her intelligence and beauty. Yet she was profoundly disinterested in the whirl of social activities available to a young debutante, instead directing her energies toward playing the piano and writing. One of her first works of fiction concerned a caged bird longing to escape, and like all of her writing it contained an autobiographical element. Some vague and seemingly indefinable need made her restless with a life that ostensibly favored her in every way.

In 1870, Kate O'Flaherty married Oscar Chopin, a young banker in St. Louis who came from a respectable Louisiana Creole family. She moved with him to Cloutierville, Louisiana where they lived on small plantations that he managed for absentee owners. They had six children and appeared to be quite happily married, but marriage did not eradicate the restlessness Chopin had felt in her teenage years. She suspected that her unhappiness had something to do with the status and choices open to women in her society.

On her honeymoon, Chopin happened to meet Tennie Claflin,

who, along with her cousin Victoria Woodhull, edited the feminist, free-love, vegetarian journal *Woodhull and Claflin's Weekly*. Claflin urged Chopin to focus her intelligence on social and political questions, and to avoid falling into the kind of mental paralysis that Claflin felt afflicted most married women of that time. Chopin promised to follow Claflin's advice, and she demonstrated her independence not only through reading and writing, but in social habits as well—smoking cigarettes and drinking beer. Most Americans considered Claflin to be little more than a meddlesome crank, but her words made sense to Kate Chopin, who tried to put them into action.

Oscar Chopin died of swamp fever in 1882, and Kate moved back to St. Louis with her six children. Under prodding of the city's famed Dr. Kolbenheyer, a free-thinking Austrian-American obstetrician, she read widely in scientific journals as well as in literary magazines. Chopin's many stories and books, including *At Fault*, *Bayou Folk*, and *A Night in Acadie*, combined Louisiana local color with frank discussions of adult female sexuality. At a time when women writers were expected to tell quaint tales about spinsters while male writers treated female sexuality as if it were the exclusive domain of lunatics or prostitutes, Chopin bucked the tide to write clearly and honestly about sexuality in a way that extended dignity to both women and men. Yet that aspect of her work did not really capture the attention of critics or the public until *The Awakening* made it impossible to avoid.

In the novel, Chopin tells the story of a woman from a border state (Kentucky in the novel) who marries into a Louisiana Creole family. Dissatisfied with her husband, she explores an affair with one young lover and actually engages in a tryst with another less honorable man. Finally, she confesses her love for the first young man, who runs away to avoid compromising her marriage. Deprived of what she wants most, she walks into the sea and drowns herself.

Like the heroine of her novel, Chopin married into a Louisiana Creole family and found herself torn between Victorian reserve and Creole sensuality. But the central theme of the novel transcended Chopin's personal circumstances to illumine a larger social issue. Nineteenth-century American society imprisoned middle- and upper-class women in idealized norms unrealistically at odds with lived experience. Physicians routinely interpreted confessions of interest in sexuality by women as evidence of gynecological disorder to be remedied by extreme methods, including clitoridectomy.

Ministers and moralists hailed women as the religious backbone of the nation and urged them to raise model children for the sake of their country, yet they ridiculed women who tried to educate themselves or to participate in politics. Women were expected to remain passive, nurturing, domestic and "decent," while men received license to act aggressively and selfishly in the world.

In that context, *The Awakening* became a *cause célèbre*. It suggested that women had the same urges and desires as men. It argued that the existing family structure did not necessarily meet those needs. It displayed sympathy for an adult woman's quest for happiness and fulfillment. As a result, some critics refused to review the book at all. Others condemned its point of view. The St. Louis Mercantile Library removed *The Awakening* from its shelves after receiving complaints, and private clubs excluded Kate Chopin from membership. Some old friends no longer found her company desirable. Deeply hurt by these rejections, Chopin retreated into her home and family and did very little additional writing before her death in 1904.

Condemned and reviled in her own day, Chopin now holds a secure place of honor in the ranks of American writers. In that big house on Morgan Street she created a novel that continues to inform and inspire all those who believe that men and women have equal rights to happiness. The title of *The Awakening* refers to the knowledge and desire for liberation growing within the novel's main character. But it applies as well to the general historical movement that Kate Chopin helped to initiate—the awakening of suppressed hopes and desires among women that has played such an important role in this century's struggles for human dignity and emancipation.

Theodore Dreiser:
An American Triumph

On a November evening in 1892, twenty-one-year-old Theodore Dreiser arrived in St. Louis to begin work as a reporter for the daily *Globe-Democrat*. As his train from Chicago pulled into the old station at Twelfth and Poplar, Dreiser fought off pangs of loneliness and fears of failure by fantasizing about what he might accomplish in his new home. Little did he realize that he would discover in St. Louis the rudiments of an art that would revolutionize the popular novel, and that all of his future work would be informed by the lessons he learned in the city.

It would be hard to imagine anyone with worse prospects for success than Dreiser when he arrived in St. Louis. Raised in poverty in a variety of midwestern cities, socially ostracized in most of them because of his family's Catholic religion, and self-conscious about his looks (he weighed less than 140 pounds even though he stood over six feet tall), Dreiser thought of himself as a perpetual outsider. He lacked the education and the family connections generally deemed necessary for a writing career in the nineteenth century, and his need to earn a living distanced him from the European "high culture" of leisure and refinement that inspired most of the literary art of his time.

Dreiser's first days in St. Louis did not exactly inspire him. Compared to Chicago he found the city "infernally dull," "sleepy," and "slow." He recoiled from the ostentatious displays of wealth by the rich with "their ridiculous money" and "brainless teas," especially when contrasted with "dreadful slums, veritably sties and warrens among the waterfronts and elsewhere . . . in which dwelt thousands upon thousands as socially forgotten as though they were dead." Even the drinking water with its peculiar yellow color upset him, as it had Mark Twain, who remarked that St. Louis tap water was too thick to drink, but too thin to plow. Indeed, the only charm Dreiser found in the city came from the inspiration he drew from recognizing that "Mark Twain had idled about here for a time, drunk and hopeless."

Yet his work for the *Globe-Democrat* enabled Dreiser to begin to see possibilities in St. Louis. The paper's editor, Joseph B. McCullagh, built a huge circulation with his combination of strong editorials praising the Republican party and judicious use of news transmitted by telegraph, enabling the *Globe* to function as a regional paper serving devoted readers as far away as Texas and Louisiana. McCullagh demanded high-quality work from his employees, and he encouraged them to write about the plurality of the city's cultures. McCullagh printed and stood behind Dreiser's favorable review of a concert by Sissieretta Jones, known as "the Black Patti," even when the other local papers then ridiculed the *Globe* for having the audacity to publicly acclaim the talents of a black woman.

Dreiser immersed himself in the richly textured urban life of St. Louis in the last decade of the nineteenth century. Part of his duties as a reporter involved covering the North Seventh Street police station, and he learned an enormous amount there about the city from police officers and criminals alike. McCullagh sent Dreiser to interview Ed Butler, the legendary ward heeler and north side political boss who had received perpetual criticism from the *Globe*'s editorial pages. Yet Butler took an immediate liking to the young reporter, offering his forgiveness in advance for anything that Dreiser's editor might later force him to write about Butler. Once Dreiser reported on a speech given to a small group of workingmen in a hall at Tenth and Walnut by Terence Powderly, the founder of the Knights of Labor. While he seriously doubted Powderly's sincerity, Dreiser approved of the labor leader's message that working people had to unite to solve their many problems.

During a stint as drama critic for the *Globe*, Dreiser saw many of the leading performers of the day, but he drew more personal satisfaction from visiting a local vaudeville hall that featured outlaw Frank James, Jesse James's elder brother, as a ticket-taker. His eclectic tastes and openness to the city's diversity sometimes had serious drawbacks. One evening Dreiser committed himself to reviewing three separate performances scheduled for the same time. Unable to be in three places at once, he simply wrote reviews of all three shows based on their press notices and went to bed without seeing any of them. This strategy backfired rather harshly when a flood washed out some railroad tracks and prevented one of the troupes from reaching St. Louis. They canceled their performance, but the next day's *Globe* carried a review by Dreiser asserting that a large and enthusiastic audience had enjoyed the production. Writers for rival papers pounced on this mistake and gleefully derided Dreiser for it. He typed up a letter of resignation and quietly slipped it onto his editor's desk so that he would not have to own up to his error in person.

Shamed by his disgrace at the *Globe*, Dreiser thought that his career as a journalist was surely over. But the city editor of the daily *Republic*, H. B. Wandell, considered Dreiser's gaffe a minor transgression, and he hired him as a feature writer. Influenced by the novels of Balzac and Zola, Wandell felt American journalism should aspire to the kind of detailed realism used so effectively by those authors. He encouraged Dreiser to imitate their style. Wandell wanted his reporters to get their facts straight, but only quickly and briefly as a prelude to more nuanced descriptions of scenery, atmosphere, and emotion.

Under Wandell's tutelage, Dreiser cultivated his understanding of and his ability to write about everyday life in the modern city. Unlike romantic writers who found beauty largely in nature, Dreiser emphasized the beauty of human emotions, especially those forged in the crucible of the urban metropolis. He wrote about the moods of the city, about the heroic and small dramas of everyday life, and about the desires and aspirations of slum dwellers—those he described as "Jewish, Negro and run-down American."

Those accounts laid the groundwork for a sensibility that Dreiser would later bring to fiction in novels including *Sister Carrie* and *An American Tragedy*. As a journalist he had learned to respect the American urban landscape with its complexities and conflicts. His ability to work them into fiction paved the way for a new kind of modern American novel. Dreiser proved that art could speak about broad concerns even when it focused on the specific details of the commonplace and ordinary, that the grandeur of the human mind and spirit does not necessarily require opulent temporal surroundings.

In his own *A Book About Myself,* Dreiser acknowledged his debts to St. Louis. Yet he never fully acclimated himself to the city. The local puritanical and conservative mores proved too confining for a young bachelor who carried on a nonstop series of love affairs almost from the moment he arrived in the city. In addition, St. Louis's significant literary culture still fell short of meeting the needs of someone with Dreiser's enormous energy and ambition. He left the city in March 1894 in search of journalistic opportunities elsewhere. He wrote for newspapers in Toledo, Cleveland, Pittsburgh, and New York before attaining success as a novelist who could fashion descriptive critiques of American life once he was freed from the constraints of daily deadlines.

As a young reporter living near the old *Globe-Democrat* offices at Sixth and Pine, Dreiser wrote bitterly about the "newly manufactured exclusivity" of private places in the Central West End. He found poetry and drama in many of the city's more desperate precincts, and the things he learned there helped to transform the future of American fiction. Dreiser titled one of his major works *An American Tragedy,* but his insistence that the rough and ordinary details of everyday life should command the attention of writers strengthened the democratic imperatives within American culture. Dreiser's achievement stands as an American triumph. It serves to remind us of the poetry and drama waiting to be recognized in the commonplace and ordinary activities of everyday life.

Scott Joplin: The King of Ragtime

In the summer of 1900, the most popular music in America came from St. Louis. Generally known as "ragtime," its appeal swept the nation. Department stores hired musicians to play it for shoppers as a way of promoting the sales of sheet music. German and Czech band leaders adapted it for performances in big-city concert halls and small-town bandshells. Middle-class families played it in their parlors on player piano rolls and wax cylinder phonograph machines. When turn-of-the-century Americans thought of music, they thought of ragtime, and when they encountered ragtime, they encountered the product of a unique moment in St. Louis history.

Ragtime originated in the taverns and social clubs of the notorious "Chestnut Valley," a red-light district along Chestnut and Market Streets near 20th. The same rough streets that inspired folktales about the "bad man" Stagger Lee and the legend of "Frankie and Johnny" gave birth to ragtime. Black musicians congregated at places like "Honest John" Turpin's Silver Dollar Saloon, the private Hurrah Sporting Club, and the parlors of madames like Mother Johnson to show off their talents for each other. They combined African-American harmonies with Euro-American marches, quadrilles, and polkas to create a complex and beautiful fusion music.

Scott Joplin arrived in St. Louis in 1885 and began playing piano in the taverns along Chestnut and Market streets. Although just seventeen years old, Joplin displayed musical gifts that belied his age. He grew up in Texarkana, Texas where his father, a former slave, worked for the railroads. His mother washed clothes for other families before being able to come home and tend to her own family. Despite their poverty, when Joplin's parents saw him playing at the church piano when he was three, they purchased one for him. Self-taught by the age of seven, young Scott Joplin attracted attention from sympathetic whites impressed by his playing. When Joplin was eleven, a German-American music teacher in Texarkana gave him free music lessons so that the world would not be deprived of the youngster's talents.

Scott Joplin's musical talent had much to offer the world, but the world was not exactly ready for him. In the late nineteenth century, the dominant form of popular music among white audiences was the "coon song," a spinoff of the minstrel shows with their racist stereotypes of blacks. White musicians who corked up their faces with blackface makeup made a fortune with songs like "All Coons

Look Alike to Me," (a song written by a black man), while black artists like Scott Joplin could not get steady work as musicians. Joplin had to follow the paths of black migrant workers wandering the lumber camps and railroad yards to find places that would hire a black musician. He left St. Louis in 1894 to seek work at the Chicago World's Fair, and eventually settled in the railroad center of Sedalia in the western part of Missouri. There he enrolled in a religious college, participated in a marching band by playing cornet, and performed on the piano late at night in a local tavern, the Maple Leaf Club.

While working at the Maple Leaf Club in 1899, Joplin composed the first hit of the ragtime genre, "The Maple Leaf Rag." Rejected by a publisher in Kansas City, Joplin brought the song to John Stark of Sedalia. Stark purchased the rights to the song for fifty dollars plus royalties to the composer—if it sold well. Within six months, Americans bought so many copies of "Maple Leaf Rag" that both Stark and Joplin had the money to move to St. Louis and set themselves up in fine homes.

Stark had served as a bugler in the Union Army during the Civil War and had later homesteaded in Missouri. A farmer and a businessman, he stumbled into the music industry as a sideline. "Maple Leaf Rag" made him one of the most important music publishers in the world. From his mansion at 3848 Washington Avenue in St. Louis, Stark supervised the printing and distribution of sheet music for ragtime songs. He built a printing plant at 3818 Laclede, and his efforts helped make St. Louis ragtime the most popular music in America. Joplin had the creative genius and the musical talent, but Stark had the capital and the white skin that brought entry into realms of the music business that Joplin could not have entered himself. Without Joplin, Stark might have remained just another member of Sedalia's middle class, but without Stark, Joplin might never have delivered his music to a wider audience.

Scott Joplin moved to 2658A Morgan Street (later renamed Delmar Boulevard) in 1900, and three years later settled in a fifteen-room house at 2117 Lucas. Freed from having to play music in "sporting houses," Joplin taught music, composed new works, and ran a boarding house. He also resumed contact with many of the musicians he had met in the Chestnut Valley in the 1880s. Just as "Honest John" Turpin's Silver Dollar Saloon had been the focal point of St. Louis ragtime in the 1880s, Turpin's son Tom presided over the city's revived musical culture at the turn of the century from his Rosebud Cafe at 2220 Market Street. At his instigation,

Joplin and other veterans interacted with a group of younger musicians to further refine the Chestnut Valley sound.

The artistry of black musicians in St. Louis at that time exceeded the opportunities presented by the commercial apparatus of the music industry. Tom Turpin wrote two hit songs, "Harlem Rag" and "St. Louis Rag," but many of his best compositions drew rejections from publishers who claimed they were too difficult for the average pianist to play. The brilliant Louis Chauvin, educated at Dumas Grade School and at Sumner High School, pioneered harmonic and rhythmic complexities that went beyond even what Scott Joplin could do, but he never succeeded in getting his compositions published. These artists envisioned new possibilities for music. They not only blended African-American and Euro-American forms, but they conceived of a music that was neither popular nor classical, but rather a blend of the two.

Joplin himself thought of his music as a new classical idiom, and admirers of his, including European classical composers Dvořák, Milhaud, and Satie, agreed. But in the United States, ragtime could win mass acceptance only within the tradition of the "coon song," with its images of "happy darkies" responding to "instinct." One crucial aspect of the minstrel show's ridicule of blacks came from caricaturing "uppity Negroes" presuming to be cultured. Whites learned to condemn black presumptions of intellect and culture on the minstrel show stage, and they proved equally resistant to its manifestations in real life. Joplin found that he could attain a modicum of fame and wealth within the ragtime genre, but he encountered unremitting resistance to his efforts to write ragtime folk ballet and opera.

In "The Ragtime Dance," Joplin designed a folk ballet, complete with a narrative soloist, orchestral accompaniment, and choreographed dancing. The piece contained nine minutes of music and took twenty minutes to perform. For three years Joplin tried unsuccessfully to convince John Stark to publish it. He eventually succeeded in 1903 only because Stark's daughter Nellie, a concert pianist, took up Joplin's cause. Yet the piece confused both distributors and the public who saw little in it but a violation of well-established popular conventions.

Undaunted, Joplin began work on an opera, "A Guest of Honor." Even though many who heard it felt that "A Guest of Honor" ranked with Joplin's best work, he never got it published. Joplin staged one performance in St. Louis in the hope of attracting capital, but was unsuccessful. Discouraged, he never even filed the opera with the

United States copyright office, and all transcripts of the work have disappeared. In 1906, Joplin left St. Louis, settling briefly in Chicago and then moving to New York. He spent the last ten years of his life on yet another ragtime opera, "Treemonisha."

Published in 1911, "Treemonisha" summarized many of the struggles of Joplin's own life and career. The story line of the opera helps explain why Joplin persisted in writing ballets and operas, and it reveals an important part of the vision that inspired all of the piano players along Chestnut and Market streets when they composed ragtime music.

The opera takes place on an Arkansas plantation, near Texarkana, in the years just after the Civil War. Ned and Monisha, a black couple, dream of having a child capable of attaining an education and living a life better their own. They find an abandoned female child and name her after Monisha, but add the prefix because they found her playing under a tree. The parents take menial jobs working for a white family—the mother washing and ironing, the father chopping wood—so that their child will have the money for an education. Armed with knowledge, Treemonisha leads her people out of ignorance and superstition so that they may obtain the good things in life. Structurally, the opera places more emphasis on the chorus than on the soloists, emphasizing Joplin's vision of progress as a collective rather than an individual matter.

The parallels between "Treemonisha" and Joplin's own life are unmistakable: the location and date of his birth, his parents' occupations, and his determination to better the status of his race through the acquisition of skills previously monopolized by whites. Nurtured by the sacrifices and high expectations of his parents, trained by classical and folk musicians, Joplin felt he had to master ballet and opera and any other "respectable" form in order to prove what black people could achieve if only given the chance.

Unfortunately, it did not work out that way. Joplin went broke trying to finance a demonstration performance of the opera in Harlem in 1915. That struggle broke his spirit, leaving him unable to fend off the effects of the illnesses (including venereal diseases) that he had picked up in the sporting houses. He brooded for long periods of time, and his piano playing deteriorated so badly that he could not even perform many of the songs he had written. Scott Joplin died in 1917, without ever seeing a staging of "Treemonisha," and deeply embittered by the neglect of his most serious works.

Today ragtime lives on in St. Louis and all across America. Nationally, recordings by Joshua Rifkin in the early 1970s, the motion picture *The Sting,* and the book and the movie *Ragtime* have revived interest in Joplin's work and career. Locally, a neighborhood group's campaign has succeeded in persuading the state of Missouri to restore Joplin's Morgan Street home as a museum and center for the study of ragtime. The great local ragtime musician and scholar, Trebor Jay Tichenor, works closely with an organization called The Friends of Scott Joplin to collect and perform ragtime pieces. But there is another part of the ragtime story that needs to be preserved. We need to remember that while Irving Berlin won plaudits for "Alexander's Ragtime Band," and while George Gershwin enjoyed acclaim for his folk opera "Porgy and Bess," Louis Chauvin and Scott Joplin were victims of a kind of cultural genocide. They died penniless without receiving recognition for their extraordinary achievements. American white racism denied them their just reward and deprived America itself of the artistic realization of its own best possibilities. We should remember as well the grand presumption and justified self-confidence of those musicians along Chestnut and Market streets who refused to let anyone tell them what they should create. Guided by a music that synthesized the insights of European and African cultures, they envisioned how great this country might become if racism no longer blinded us to the talent, character, and dignity of each individual.

Felix Carvajal:
Hero of the 1904 Olympics

In 1904, St. Louis commanded the attention of the world. The city hosted a World's Fair, the Democratic party's national convention, and the most unusual Olympic Games of the modern era. The highly successful Louisiana Purchase Exposition and the Democratic National Convention would be considered triumphs even today, but the Olympics of 1904 scarcely resembled what we have come to expect from the quadrennial pinnacle of athletic competition. As the first Olympic competition staged outside of Europe, the Games in St. Louis attracted fewer than five hundred athletes from just a handful of countries. They competed before small crowds under less than ideal conditions. Yet the 1904 Olympiad may have remained truer to the ideals of international competition than the lavishly subsidized and highly nationalistic contests of recent years.

No one individual embodied the peculiar nature of the 1904 Games better than its unlikely hero, Felix Carvajal. A postman from Havana who fancied himself as a world-class marathon runner, Carvajal financed his trip to St. Louis by running exhibition races in the streets of his home country. Excited by Carvajal's confidence and engaged by his audacity, patriotic Cubans gave him funds for passage to St. Louis so that he could represent their newly independent nation in the Olympics.

Unfortunately, Carvajal stopped off in New Orleans on his way to the Games. He tried to increase his supply of cash at some of that city's more notorious gambling establishments, and he soon lost every cent that he had brought with him from Cuba. Carvajal had to hitchhike all the way to St. Louis, arriving just in time for the start of the competition. The Cuban begged other athletes for lodging and food, and won the sympathy of a group of American weight lifters who let him stay in their rooms and adopted him as their "mascot."

On August 30, Felix Carvajal lined up for the twenty-six-plus-mile marathon race on a ninety-degree St. Louis summer day. Unlike the other runners who competed in track shoes and running shorts, the postman from Havana began the race in street shoes with heavy heels, long trousers, a long-sleeved shirt, and his favorite hat—a dapper beret. At one point during the race his hunger caught up with him, so Carvajal jumped a fence and ate green apples in a conveniently located orchard. Jumping back into the race, he took the lead and appeared headed for certain victory. But a combination of the summer heat, green apples, and lack of adequate rest and nutrition took its toll. Carvajal stumbled back into the pack. Incredibly, he still mustered the strength to finish in fourth place, not quite good enough for a medal, but sufficient to establish him as a hero among fans, writers, and fellow athletes.

The marathon race featured another unusual occurrence. Fred Lorz of the United States appeared to be the winner of the gold medal when he crossed the finish line well ahead of the other runners. But when suspicious judges raised questions about his extraordinarily fast time, Lorz confessed that he had received an important assist from a passing motorist. Finding himself falling behind early in the race, Lorz flagged down an unsuspecting automobile driver along the route, riding most of the distance to the finish line in that car. Other runners had seen Lorz fall behind, and none of them saw him pass them. Yet they found themselves behind him at the finish. The judges awarded the gold medal to the second-place finisher, who, as far as we know, ran the whole course himself.

One other oddity added a vulgar and tasteless aura to the competition: Anthropology Days at the Games. Olympic officials contacted some of the aboriginal peoples "on display" at the World's Fair, and arranged for them to compete in contests purportedly scaled to their skills. Ainus from Japan and Pygmies from Africa competed in one-time-only Olympic events like the pole climb and the mud fight. Yet for all of the farce connected with the marathon and with Anthropology Days, some events provided incidents of real drama and accomplishment. Contestants broke Olympic and world records in the high jump, shot put and discus throw, with athletic clubs from the United States turning in especially good performances. A Canadian policeman won one gold medal in a field event, but every other gold medal went to contestants from the United States. George Poage, representing the Milwaukee Athletic Club, became the first black man to compete in the modern Olympic Games and the first to win a medal, placing third in the four-hundred-meter hurdles.

In addition to the success of American athletes, the 1904 Olympics contributed to the international stature of the United States by placing St. Louis on a par with the previous sites of the games, Athens and Paris. The athletic competition and the World's Fair enhanced the image of the city and the nation, and the spirit of fellowship and competition as exemplified by Felix Carvajal fulfilled the highest elements of the Olympic ideal.

Of course, contestants in the modern Olympics have far surpassed the performances of those in 1904. No women competed in the St. Louis Games, and the athletes who did attend represented only ten nations. Carvajal paid his own way to the Games, but as his desperate need for cash indicated, the standards of amateurism guiding the Olympic movement generally restricted participation to athletes from wealthier countries. In addition, better training methods, superior equipment, and improved facilities have ensured ever-better performances and healthier athletes in the modern era.

Yet the 1904 Olympics proceeded free from drug abuse, national chauvinism, or under-the-table payments to professionals masquerading as amateurs. Athletes participated in those games for the rewards of competition measured in degrees of self-discipline and self-respect, rather than in quantities of self-aggrandizing commercial endorsements. Competitors from one nation opened their camp to a penniless Cuban postman, not as a national rival, but as a fellow athlete.

By contemporary standards, we would have to judge the St. Louis

Olympics an artistic and commercial failure. But today's carefully programmed athletes and partisan nationalistic fans could do worse than to emulate the dogged determination of Felix Carvajal or the gracious sportsmanship of the athletes and fans who took him to their hearts in St. Louis in 1904.

Josephine Baker: Le Jazz Hot

Josephine Baker went from the slums of St. Louis to international stardom. She grew up in a one-room shack but owned a thirty-room mansion in a Paris suburb while still in her twenties. Baker remained a celebrity for six decades; her dancing, singing, and acting made her one of the most beloved entertainers of all time. Yet she never forgot the suffering of her youth, and risked everything at the peak of her popularity to battle fearlessly for human rights all over the world.

Born in 1906, Josephine Baker grew up near the corner of Targee and Gratiot, in the Mill Creek Valley on the near south side of St. Louis. She sneaked into the train yards near Union Station late at night to steal coal so that her family could stay warm, and she scavenged through garbage cans at Soulard Market so they could have enough to eat. Baker attended Lincoln Elementary School near her home, but she received her real education from musicians who played in the taverns, dance halls, and theatres of her neighborhood. Their artistic creations inspired her, and their stories about travel to faraway places, money, and fame stimulated her ambitions.

No one could have predicted that this skinny, buck-toothed, impoverished black child would one day become an international sex symbol receiving more than forty thousand love letters and some two thousand marriage proposals before her twenty-first birthday. Josephine Baker did her first performing on sidewalks outside the Booker T. Washington Theatre, begging for pennies from patrons waiting on line to see the professional revues inside the theatre. She played tunes on a comb covered with tissue paper and on a home-made banjo made out of a cigar box and rubber bands. Gradually, she worked her way first into a family vaudeville act, then into the chorus line of musical shows, and then into supporting roles as a singer and dancer providing comic relief for the main acts.

Determined to succeed in show business, Baker carefully copied the songs and dance steps of the stars. She learned their lines and songs secretly, hoping that if the stars became ill, she might be asked to stand in for them. One such occasion led to her big break—a singing and dancing appearance that landed her a spot in "Shuffle Along," an all-black musical written by Eubie Blake and Noble Sissle that opened in New York in 1921. Four years later, Baker found herself in Paris, a show business sensation as the lead exotic dancer in the Folies-Bergere revue.

Parisian audiences went crazy over Baker's "exotic" beauty and uninhibited eroticism. She appeared nearly nude in production numbers designed to exploit sexist and racist European fantasies connecting black women with primitive lust and sensuality. Yet Europe nonetheless offered opportunities for stardom denied to a dark-skinned woman in America, and Baker took advantage of her fame to launch a diversified acting career that included roles in many European motion pictures. She became a popular celebrity as well as an acquaintance and confidante of intellectuals, including the theatre director Max Reinhardt, the scientist Albert Einstein, and the well-known architect Le Corbusier.

French writers celebrated "La Ba-Kair" as the essence of the spirit of hot jazz. To a continent demoralized by World War I and battered by economic reverses, Josephine Baker stood out as an affirmation of life, as a celebration of joy in the face of great suffering. She returned the affection given to her by the French people, adopting Paris as her home and working for a variety of patriotic French organizations. In the late 1930s, with the outbreak of war looming ever more likely, she accepted a dangerous assignment from the French government to use her contacts at the Italian Embassy in Paris to spy on the Fascist Mussolini government.

World War II started in 1939, and in 1940 Paris fell to the Nazis. Baker fled to North Africa where she worked for the Free French government-in-exile. She scorned turncoat collaborationist entertainers like Maurice Chevalier who remained in Paris to "celebrate" the joys of the city under Nazi occupation. Baker served as a sublieutenant in the Free French Army and after the war received the Rosette of the Resistance in honor of her practical contributions and her symbolic importance to the anti-Fascist cause in France.

Her wartime experiences convinced Josephine Baker that everyone had a moral obligation to combat racism. Her personal successes in the 1920s meant nothing to those who considered her part of an inferior race. Millions lacking her resources went to their deaths in gas chambers because of the racist Nazi ideology. She vowed to devote her energies in the postwar era to an all-out battle against race hatred. Part of that battle meant returning to the United

States and confronting the racism and segregation that her fame and stardom in Europe had enabled her to escape for so long.

As a child growing up in St. Louis, Baker had witnessed racism firsthand. By referendum in 1916, city voters institutionalized residential segregation by making it illegal for blacks and whites to move onto blocks that already had a majority of the other race. Although eventually overturned by the courts, the referendum expressed the enormity of race hatred on the local level. In 1917, whites in East St. Louis rioted against blacks seeking jobs in war industries, systematically burning down black-owned houses, and killing and brutalizing people of color. Years later Baker recalled for interviewers how she watched as the mob clubbed to death one of her friends and burned alive a black woman in a Packard automobile. Baker ran away from that madness as a young woman, but at the age of forty-five, she decided to come home and confront it head-on.

Josephine Baker's return to the United States in 1951 produced both personal and professional triumphs. Her insistence on performing exclusively before integrated groups broke the color barrier that had previously divided audiences in many big cities, including Miami. She refused to perform at the Chase Hotel in St. Louis for $12,000 a week because that establishment refused to abide by her rules about integrating the audience. But she did return to St. Louis to appear for free at a rally organized by the NAACP and by Harold Gibbons of the Teamsters Union calling for desegregation of local schools.

As the civil rights movement gained momentum, Josephine Baker gained stature as one of its main proponents and patrons. She secretly funded the legal defense of a black truck driver in Mississippi who was executed on what many knew to be unsubstantiated charges of raping a white woman. She loaned her name, her time, and her resources to many civil rights causes. In order to show that different races could live in peace, she brought fourteen children of different nationalities into her home and adopted them as members of her "rainbow family."

Josephine Baker died in Paris in 1975, and was mourned all over the world. She was a woman who clawed her way out of excruciating poverty into worldwide fame and wealth. She rose to international fame by shaking her nearly naked body to play to the racist and sexist fantasies of European men, but she then turned herself into a dignified crusader for human rights. Her personal transformations and triumphs resonate with the wisdom she expressed to

James Farmer of the Congress of Racial Equality when that organization received much criticism for its militance in the 1960s. Baker's message to Farmer and the message of her life to us are one and the same—"Courage, courage to all of you. Complete victory is not far away."

W. C. Handy: The Birth of Our Blues

For more than seventy years, "St. Louis Blues" has been one of the most popular songs in the world. It has been recorded more than five hundred times, inspired three motion pictures, and even served as a battle hymn for the Ethiopian Army. It is one of the few songs to have been recorded by both the "Big Band" stylist Tex Beneke and the rock and roll artist Chuck Berry, and may be the only song with a professional hockey team named after it. (Unless of course, one counts the ill-fated decision some years ago to name the minor league hockey team in Macon, Georgia the "Macon Whoopies.")

Curiously enough, this song, which has done so much to establish the reputation of St. Louis as a center for the blues, is not strictly a blues number and was composed in Memphis by a man whose experience in St. Louis consisted of only a few unhappy weeks. In September 1914, forty-year-old William C. Handy locked himself into a rented room in Memphis with the intention of forcing himself to write a song. Handy led a small black jazz ensemble popular in Memphis's dance halls. Two years previous he had written the highly successful "Memphis Blues." Unfortunately, chronic poverty forced Handy to sell the publishing rights to that song for fifty dollars, depriving him of its substantial subsequent earnings. Pressed for money once again, Handy hoped to write a tune that would make it easier to take care of his wife and four children, who suffered under the burden of his meager earnings as a musician. With a bottle of liquor by his side, Handy searched his memory for some experience that might serve as the basis for a song.

Twenty-one years earlier, Handy had spent two weeks in St. Louis looking for work. He had started out for Chicago intent on playing his music at the World's Fair, but when the Fair was postponed for a year he went to St. Louis because of its reputation as a place where musicians could always find work. But the financial panic of 1893 hit the city hard, and there was little work to be found.

"I slept in a vacant lot at Twelfth and Morgan streets, a lot I shared with a hundred others in similar circumstances," he later recalled. Handy also slept on the cobblestones underneath the Eads Bridge, and he wandered throughout the city wearing a frayed coat with no shirt underneath. He had long tried to forget that unhappy period in his life, but as he sat in his rented room in Memphis, the experience came back to him. He thought about himself as he had been in 1893: cold, poor, unshaven, and hungry. He remembered looking in the windows of taverns and restaurants that he could not afford to enter. Suddenly, he recalled someone who had seemed even more miserable in St. Louis than he had been, a woman who walked along the levee crying that her man "had a heart like a rock cast in the sea." Handy's memories of her misery and of his own unhappiness blended together, and they inspired Handy to write the "St. Louis Blues."

Starting with the traditional three-line, twelve-bar blues, Handy set them in a minor key, adding a tango rhythm and a sixteen-bar section to make the song more contemporary and more commercial. He based the chorus on a three-note phrase he remembered hearing when he was growing up in Florence, Alabama—a phrase that he had used previously in a song which he called "Jogo Blues," but which he published as "The Memphis Itch." By morning, Handy had combined these bits and pieces of his memories and experiences into the "St. Louis Blues."

Excited by his new composition, Handy stayed awake all day and scored the song for his band so that they could play it in a dance hall that evening. He walked outside and sat at the counter of Pee Wee's Cigar Stand on Memphis's famed Beale Street for most of the day, writing the parts for each instrument. When Handy and his ensemble introduced the song to the world that night, the composer knew immediately from the dancers' enthusiasm that he had a hit song.

Music publishers did not share Handy's optimism about the "St. Louis Blues." They thought of the blues as a rural style with little appeal for urban audiences, dismissing the popularity of "Memphis Blues" as a fluke. Even the popular elements in the song, like the tango rhythm, failed to convince them that it would be commercially successful. So Handy published the tune himself, paying for copyright and printing costs out of advance sales of sheet music to department stores. Eventually, "St. Louis Blues" earned more than two million dollars for the composer and his family.

Ironically, the popularity of "St. Louis Blues" contributed to the demise of St. Louis as a center of the music industry. Even though the first scored twelve-bar blues had been published in St. Louis in 1904, local publisher John Stark rejected "St. Louis Blues" as too primitive to have much appeal for urban audiences. By the time Stark realized his error, the blues had already supplanted ragtime as the cutting edge of popular music. Stark held a contest to attract blues composers to his publishing house, but, with the exception of the very popular "Weary Blues," he experienced no particular success, and publishers in other cities came to dominate the blues market.

Handy's "St. Louis Blues" brought dynamic changes to popular music. White artists began to mine the blues tradition for ideas and inspiration, and Paul Whiteman became the "King of Jazz" in the 1920s by playing only slightly modified arrangements of compositions by black musicians like W. C. Handy. Blues chord progressions, harmonies, and lyrical patterns became so influential that they provided the basic foundation for most American popular music for decades to come. Once Mamie Smith's "Crazy Blues" established her as one of the preeminent recording artists of the 1920s, other black blues singers, like St. Louis's Lonnie Johnson and Victoria Spivey, found opportunities for commercial success.

Bessie Smith's 1925 recording of "St. Louis Blues" inspired one of the three films named after the song. Smith's appearance in this short 1928 film provides the only permanent visual record of her monumental talent, and it is still shown today to jazz fans and scholars. In 1939, Paramount Pictures made a full-length, but largely forgettable version of *St. Louis Blues* with Dorothy Lamour. The best film based on the song appeared in 1958 when Nat "King" Cole starred in a biography of Handy. Despite a mediocre script and pedestrian production, stunning musical performances by Cole, Eartha Kitt, Cab Calloway, Pearl Bailey, Mahalia Jackson, and Barney Bigard made the 1958 *St. Louis Blues* a memorable film and an important cultural artifact.

The 1958 film also gave St. Louis an opportunity to bring Handy back to the city. Local political leaders and Hollywood studio executives arranged to stage the film's premiere in St. Louis and to honor Handy for his role in spreading the city's fame through his song. But the composer died suddenly in his New York home at the age of 84, just ten days before the scheduled premiere. St. Louis marked the film's opening with a dignified ceremony at Soldier's Memorial instead, and St. Louis Jazz expert Charlie Menees authored a moving and perceptive tribute to Handy in the *Post-Dispatch*.

Over the years, many great artists have worked slices of St. Louis life into their art. Mark Twain, Theodore Dreiser, Kate Chopin, T. S. Eliot, Jack Conroy, and Tennessee Williams have all won deserved fame and recognition for art fashioned from life in St. Louis. W. C. Handy's contribution is no less important. It took him twenty-one years and one inspired night of composition to turn his experiences into art, but because he did, St. Louis, and the composer who immortalized it, became known all over the world.

Bix and Tram:
The Roaring Twenties in St. Louis

In the summer of 1925, Bix Beiderbecke moved to St. Louis. He took up residence in Room 608 at the Coronado Hotel on Lindell, just west of Grand. He arrived as a handsome, intelligent, and successful twenty-two-year-old man. When he left the city a year later, he had achieved recognition as one of the great geniuses of American music. The story of Bix Beiderbecke's year in St. Louis makes up an important chapter in the history of popular music, and it reveals much about the kinds of creativity that flowered in American cities during the 1920s.

Born to a wealthy family in Davenport, Iowa in 1903, Leon Bismarck Beiderbecke received a characteristically German-American musical education on the piano and the cornet. After struggling through high school and the Lake Forest Military Academy, he finally convinced his parents and teachers that his interests lay outside the realm of formal education. The cornet was Bix's major preoccupation, especially as he heard it played by jazz musicians on the riverboats in Davenport and on weekend escapes from prep school to Chicago night clubs. In 1923, Beiderbecke formed his own jazz band, the Wolverines. When they disbanded, he came to St. Louis in order to play in the orchestra of local saxophone player Frankie Trumbauer.

Known to his friends as Tram, Trumbauer grew up in southern Illinois and later lived at 2304a Russell in south St. Louis. Short, wiry, and quiet, he made quite a contrast with the tall, robust, good-looking and extroverted Beiderbecke. But on the bandstand, the two meshed perfectly. They were both white midwesterners obsessed with the music of black New Orleans, and their group became a big local favorite playing dances at Tremps Bar on Delmar and at the Arcadia Ballroom on Olive—just a few blocks from the

Coronado Hotel. In Trumbauer's band, Beiderbecke found steady work, appreciative fans, artistic challenges, and most important of all, access to the rich musical cultures of St. Louis.

Beiderbecke combated the loneliness of life in a new city by attending St. Louis Symphony concerts with a friend, jazz pianist Bud Hassler. At the symphony he learned new harmonic ideas from the works of composers like Claude Debussy and Igor Stravinsky. After the concerts, Beiderbecke and Hassler would seek out pianos in deserted bars where they would experiment with the sounds they had just heard. Beiderbecke's beautiful neoclassical composition, "In a Mist," grew out of these excursions.

Yet the most important part of Bix's musical education came after-hours. Following a full night's work at the Arcadia, Westlake Park, Tremps Hall, or one of the other dance halls reserved exclusively for white musicians and dancers, Beiderbecke and Trumbauer habitually walked over to the black night clubs in the Mill Creek Valley like John Estes's Chauffeur's Club on West Pine. There they could hear the music that had drawn them to jazz in the first place.

At the black night clubs, Beiderbecke began to understand what could be done with his horn, with free improvisation and rapid jumps and falloffs in octaves. Alone in his room, he practiced everything he heard. He found that the stalest cliché at the Chauffeur's Club could bring down the house at the Arcadia. Beiderbecke gained an enthusiastic following among white jazz fans for playing music that they could have heard everywhere if segregation had not limited black artists to mostly black audiences. Bix could not play publicly with black musicians, but he could learn from their creativity and bring their messages to new audiences.

For a man devoted to music, St. Louis in 1925 offered an ideal site as a meeting ground for Euro-American classical and African-American popular musics. Beiderbecke became so absorbed in music that he would go for weeks without changing his clothes or cleaning his room. Only Trumbauer's nagging could induce Beiderbecke to pay any attention at all to his domestic life. Except for his fascination with major league baseball and the Browns and Cardinals games at nearby Sportsman's Park, Beiderbecke devoted all of his time and energy to music.

Because of the things he had heard at the symphony, Beiderbecke refined his skills at reading sheet music. Because of his passion for African-American music, he fully developed his improvisational techniques. By the summer of 1926, his skills and talents led him out of St. Louis and into the Jean Goldkette and Paul Whiteman orchestras. Joining the Goldkette aggregation in May 1926, Bix spent that summer with them in Hudson, Indiana at the Blue Lantern Inn. Trumbauer and the St. Louis clarinetist, Pee Wee Russell, joined the band as well, and they continued the musical explorations they had initiated in St. Louis. Russell and Beiderbecke shared a cabin where they spent the days playing the piano, eating canned beans and sardines, and sampling the Prohibition era's finest bootleg liquor.

The Goldkette Orchestra dissolved in October 1927, causing Beiderbecke and Trumbauer to sign up with the "King of Jazz," Paul Whiteman, and his Orchestra. They experienced unprecedented financial rewards with Whiteman, but their artistry suffered. The "King of Jazz" tolerated neither the improvisational devices of African-American music nor the harmonic complexities of modern symphonic music. Beiderbecke had to swallow his pride and play the watered-down and over-arranged melodies that most of the public and Paul Whiteman understood as jazz.

Some others fared worse; Duke Ellington and Louis Armstrong had to go to Europe to find audiences truly receptive to their music. Beiderbecke stayed in the Whiteman band and watched his dream of a fundamentally new, hybrid music die from commercial neglect. Retreating into alcohol and his libertine lifestyle, Beiderbecke died on August 7, 1931. The official health record cites pneumonia as the cause of death, but as a former classmate of his explained, "He died of everything." He was twenty-eight years old.

Even to this day, Beiderbecke's records sell reasonably well. A festival in Davenport, Iowa every summer commemorates his life and his influence on jazz. But in St. Louis, the memories of Bix have faded. The Coronado Hotel now serves as a dormitory for St. Louis University, and the Arcadia Ballroom and the Chauffeur's Club are long gone. But when we walk the streets that he walked, we might want to remember the wealthy, young white man drawn to the culture of working-class blacks, the wild-living jazz musician who spent his afternoons at the symphony. Beiderbecke understood that these worlds were not so far apart, that everyone has something to offer others, and that the best cultures are those that are fused from the contributions of everyone.

Billy Peek: Let it Rock

He is too young to be a historical figure, but he is also too important to leave out of history. Billy Peek is a St. Louis institution, a living legend who writes the history of his city with the music he plays on his guitar. He learned his craft listening to St. Louis blues musicians, including Albert King, Ike Turner, and the great Chuck Berry. Then he went on to international recognition as a rock and roll musician for his work with Rod Stewart's band. But wherever Billy Peek goes, he takes a little of St. Louis with him in the hard-driving, boogie-woogie rock and roll that he says "tells a story and tells it in overdrive."

"I grew up on a street called Tower Grove," he explains when asked about his origins as a musician, adding that "it was a good environment to grow up in to finally become a rock and roll musician because it had all the background that it needed to give that good time feeling." Tower Grove Avenue between Chouteau and Vandeventer formed the main corridor through "The Grove," a south side working-class neighborhood where Peek grew up in the 1940s and 1950s. Like many people in the neighborhood, his parents had migrated from southeast Missouri during World War II to look for work in the foundries, warehouses, and slaughterhouses along the Frisco Railroad tracks. They worked hard all day, and at night they relaxed to the sounds of country music singers, like Ernest Tubb and Red Foley, coming from the radio and from jukeboxes around town.

Billy Peek learned to play country music on the guitar at home, and his neighborhood provided him with other resources. At Adams Elementary School and Roosevelt High School he met people who would remain his friends for life. One summer when he was a teenager, all of his friends got Mohawk haircuts and formed a club called the Mohawks. "Nobody's parents were too pleased with that," he remembers, but it was the kind of neighborhood where everyone stuck together and everyone felt a part of something.

One day at a corner candy store, Billy ran into the hippest guy in the neighborhood, the one who was always "in the know" before anyone else. Snapping his fingers and wearing an Ivy League cap, he motioned Billy over to the jukebox and said, "Hey man, wait 'til you hear this." He played Chuck Berry's "Maybelline," and it changed Billy Peek's life. "I liked what I heard immediately," he remembers, and he knew then he would make his living playing it. "I could stand on my head all day long and play that style," he says of Chuck Berry's music. Other guitar players might try to learn the notes, but Billy Peek had the feel of this music from the start. When he heard that Chuck Berry was from St. Louis he could hardly believe it. He set out on a quest to hear this music played by its true originators.

Billy Peek went to the Club Imperial in north St. Louis to hear Ike Turner, and he went over to East St. Louis to the Midtown Country Club, the Apollo Club, the Palladium, and the Plantation to hear Little Milton and Albert King. On Tuesday nights he would sit in with Ike Turner's band and play the "Okie Dokie Stomp" to show off his skill. As a white teenager trying to make an impression playing with a black band, Peek would play the song twice as fast as Ike Turner did, a demonstration that won applause from the crowd but which caused more than a little grumbling on the part of Turner's drummer who hated to have to play that fast.

It was an exciting time for St. Louis music. Chuck Berry, who had lived his whole life in the highly segregated Ville neighborhood in the heart of black St. Louis, all of a sudden found himself playing all over town and drawing white teenagers to his appearances. A creative new synthesis emerged from the search by young whites for an exciting music that they could call their own. As Billy Peek recalls, "For so long black artists had been entertaining and doing this type of thing we didn't know anything about. I'm saying we, as the white community, didn't know anything about it until they started making some records and the kids started buying them and they found out 'Hey, these guys are playing some out-of-sight music.'"

Like many other white teenagers, Billy Peek listened to disc jockeys Dave Dixon on KATZ and Jesse "Spider" Burks on KXLW to hear blues and rock and roll. He learned the language of the blues and tried it out on his guitar—the one-string runs of B. B. King, the bottleneck sound of Elmore James, and the 8/8 time rolling bass boogie-woogie of Muddy Waters that became the subtext of American rock and roll. But the most important influence on Peek remained Chuck Berry.

Three years after he heard "Maybelline" in that corner candy store, Billy Peek played on the bill at a show featuring Chuck Berry. Peek had previously pulled off a successful appearance on Russ Carter's "St. Louis Hop," and as a result was chosen to appear on that program's first anniversary show, at the Casa Loma Ballroom on Iowa near Cherokee in south St. Louis. Peek was the warm-up act, and he was careful not to steal the headliner's thunder, so he played no Chuck Berry songs that night. But he did meet his hero and get his autograph, which was thrilling enough. Before long, the two would be playing together. In the early 1960s, Peek worked at the Terrace Lounge on the DeBaliviere strip, playing his entire repertoire of rock and roll songs, but doing especially well with Chuck Berry's material. Late in 1963, Berry strolled into the club and liked what he heard. Soon, he arranged for Peek to play at Berry Park in Wentzville on Sunday afternoons. Peek played some Ray Charles songs, a few B. B. King numbers, a little of Jimmy Reed's tunes, and nearly everything ever done by Chuck Berry. Sometimes Berry would sit in with Peek's group, and they would play together. The years at Berry Park enabled Billy Peek to get close to Chuck Berry, musically and personally, and that association later led to a European tour during which Peek played in Berry's backup band.

In 1973, Billy Peek backed up Chuck Berry on a tour of Europe, and he began to see that he could hold his own with guitarists from all over the world. They played together again in 1975 on an awards show honoring Berry's induction into the rock and roll Hall of Fame, and shortly after that on the television show "Rock Concert." Rod Stewart happened to see that show with his guitarist Ron Wood, and Wood suggested that Peek would be perfect for the new band that Stewart intended to form.

When he auditioned for Rod Stewart, Billy Peek drew upon all that he had learned growing up in the Grove. Stewart asked him to listen to one of the tracks they had recorded and to play whatever came into his head. The number they asked him to accompany was "The Wild Side of Life," a Hank Thompson country song that Billy's father used to play around the house and that Billy used to play at his parents' tavern, the "Peek-a-boo" on Tower Grove Avenue. Billy laid down a hard-driving Chuck Berry–style rhythm underneath the melody, and when he saw Rod Stewart jump in the air and scream, "That's exactly what I want, that's it!" he knew he had the job. Stewart's band had been struggling with that number, but for a guitarist who grew up in the Grove it posed no problem.

Billy Peek played in Rod Stewart's band for five years, starring with solos on "Hot Legs" and "Ball Trap." His music is an encyclopedia of blues and rock and roll licks, with a little bit of country and a lot of the Grove mixed in. It's music that comes from lived experience, from feelings that can't be created artificially.

"I've always been a rock and roll player, and I'll always be a rock and roll player, " Peek proclaims. "And blues, I think the older I get, the more I lean toward blues. And I'm even giving thoughts about leaning into country music a little, because I'm beginning to find out what my Dad was talking about." Billy Peek knows that rock and roll is not a separate form, but a fusion of working-class musics including the blues and the country music that came together at a very special time in history. In neighborhoods like the Grove and the Ville, white and black musicians crossed barriers that had divided them for centuries, and they created a powerful new American music.

When we hear Billy Peek play and sing we hear a great technician and a great artist. But we also hear about a part of the past that is worth nurturing and preserving, not just in music, but in the social and political life of the larger community whose interactions gave life to the music in the first place.

Politics

Revolution in Haiti:
How St. Louis Joined the United States

When the English established their first permanent settlement in North America, in Virginia in 1607, the Osage and the Missouri Indians controlled the land that is now St. Louis. When the British subjects of Massachusetts executed suspected witches in the 1690s, France claimed sovereignty over all the land bordering the Mississippi River. When George Washington led the American Revolution, Spain held firm control over St. Louis. It was not until 1803 that the city became part of the United States, and then it was not because of anything that happened locally but rather because of events far away in the Caribbean and in Europe.

Thomas Jefferson's purchase of the Louisiana Territory from Napoleon Bonaparte brought St. Louis into the United States. The two leaders made the deal in response to circumstances beyond their control, circumstances caused by the one man most responsible for Haitian independence, (and in a roundabout way for making St. Louis a part of the United States)—a Haitian slave named Toussaint L'Ouverture.

Unlike Jefferson or Bonaparte, Toussaint did not make his mark on the world as a young man. Working as a slave on a Haitian plantation until he was forty-five, Toussaint found himself entrusted with no more responsibility than stewardship over livestock. But like Jefferson and Bonaparte, the worldwide revolutionary ferment of the last half of the eighteenth century drew him into public life. When the French Revolution commenced in 1789, Toussaint immediately recognized the possibilities it presented for himself and for other oppressed people, and he took up arms on behalf of the revolutionary forces in the French colony where he lived. For twelve years, he fought for the revolution and against slavery, ultimately winning independence for his country from France.

As a slave, Toussaint had enjoyed a more favored position as a livestock steward than those slaves cutting sugar cane in the fields. He used his advantages to learn about the world, reading Caesar's *Commentaries* and other classic works of European civilization. During trips to the cities for his owners, he absorbed political ideas by listening to the debates among whites and mulattoes about the island's future. Toussaint also displayed impressive physical skills in running, swimming, and riding. Even at the age of sixty, he reputedly continued to ride his horse one hundred twenty-five miles a day. These innate mental and physical characteristics took on historical importance when Toussaint applied them effectively both in political action and in battle.

Toussaint emerged as the military and political leader of slaves in Haiti. Under his command, they fought to make Haiti an independent part of the French Republic. Then they fought for six years to expel British troops attempting to exploit the chaos of the French Revolution by capturing the colony's riches for the British crown. When Napoleon came to power in France in 1799, he decided that he had to subdue Toussaint and reestablish French control over the Haitian economy and government.

Napoleon's armies had stormed from success to success in Europe, but the campaign in Haiti proved to be a different matter. Malaria and other diseases afflicted the French soldiers, while the uneducated and ill-fed troops under Toussaint's leadership proved more than a match for the most successful army in European history. Combat-tested against the British and fighting on their own territory for their own freedom, the Haitians defeated the French in a bloody and costly war that depleted Napoleon's army and drained the French treasury.

Toussaint's successful war for independence left Napoleon desperate. He withdrew his troops in order to deploy them back to Europe, and he went looking for ways to raise money. The Louisiana territory, including St. Louis, offered his only hope, so he acquired it from Spain via a complicated treaty. The Spaniards had discovered that they could not afford to defend their vast holdings in both South and North America. They had invited Americans and other settlers into St. Louis and other underpopulated parts of their northern territories, even offering them immunity from taxation if they settled under the Spanish flag. But the policy worked too well, and Spain feared that too much American settlement in its territories might ultimately threaten Texas and Mexico, as indeed it did.

Unable to support or defend its northern territory, Spain transferred title of the land to Napoleon on the condition that he grant the Spanish the right of first refusal if he ever wanted to sell the land to some other country. Originally Napoleon had conceived of North America as just another region in his grand strategy of conquest, but the losses he suffered at Toussaint's hands made him change his mind and think of it instead as a source of revenue.

When Thomas Jefferson learned of Louisiana's transfer to France, he feared for the safety and navigation rights of American settlers in the west. The president sent a delegation, headed by James Monroe, to purchase the city of New Orleans and strategic parts of West Florida in order to safeguard American commerce in the Gulf of Mexico. To their surprise, Napoleon offered to sell the entire Louisiana territory to the United States for only $15 million.

Jefferson had traditionally opposed any territorial expansion, arguing that presidents should only exercise powers expressly given to them in the Constitution. Yet he reversed himself on both issues when the opportunity to acquire Louisiana came his way. Jefferson had no specifically articulated constitutional right to buy the property, but then again, Napoleon had no specific right to sell it. The French dictator clearly violated his promises to the Spaniards, but by that time there was nothing that they could do about it. Overnight, the transaction doubled the size of the United States. It changed the future of world politics, and it delivered St. Louis from Spain to the United States.

Many ironic developments transpired to provoke the Louisiana Purchase. Haiti brought Napoleon his first defeat, even though it was the first time that his troops fought with material advantages over their enemy. France held a clear edge over the Haitians in men and munitions, but Toussaint borrowed a page from Bonaparte's book by rallying his troops behind the ideals of liberty and equality. French troops thought of themselves as a revolutionary army freeing captive peoples from aristocratic rule in every other place they fought, but in Haiti they knew that their opponents carried the banner of liberation, with disastrous consequences for French morale.

For Americans in St. Louis, the transfer of power from Spain to the United States brought unexpected anxiety. Monarchist Spain had given them free land, exempted them from taxes, and left them alone. They could hardly expect such favored treatment from the democratic republic that now commanded their allegiance. For slaves, the transfer held an even greater irony. Instead of living under the ambiguous and weak slave codes of Spain, they found themselves living in a country whose Constitution clearly protected slavery and expressly reduced them to the status of property.

Toussaint freed his own people, and he had a lasting impact on world politics. Ultimately betrayed into Napoleon's hands, he died in captivity in France, never living to see the freedom he fought so valiantly to secure for others. In nations around the world he is remembered as the first colonial victor against European imperialism, and as proof that the will to freedom lives on even, or perhaps especially, in the hearts of slaves.

In St. Louis, the Toussaint L'Ouverture public school honors the city's indirect patron, but he is entitled to more. The Lacledes and Chouteaus and Jeffersons all receive their due as benefactors of St. Louis, as historical figures whose actions helped lay the groundwork for the present. The ex-slave whose heroic efforts won independence for his own country and brought St. Louis into the United States deserves the same status. In an interdependent world, even emperors sometimes capitulate to slaves, and local heroes can sometimes come from very far away.

The Plow That Broke Their Plans: Cultural Geography and Local Leadership

Nothing aggravated nineteenth-century St. Louis civic leaders more than the rise of Chicago as the dominant industrial and commercial center of the Midwest. St. Louis boasted seventy years of settlement, well-developed transportation facilities, and sophisticated business leadership before Chicago even incorporated itself as a city in 1833. Yet the Illinois metropolis soon equaled or surpassed St. Louis in every major category of population and trade. Chicago's superiority set the agenda for generations of civic leaders in St. Louis, but even the most herculean efforts could not reverse the tide.

Nearly every civic or commercial improvement in St. Louis after 1840 was justified by the necessity of competition with Chicago. The Missouri Legislature granted a charter to the Pacific Railroad in 1849 for a western route across the state, in hopes of keeping Chicago from dominating trade with the west coast. Similarly, while St. Louisans had discussed a railroad bridge across the Mississippi River as early as 1839, they did not build the Eads Bridge until three rail lines serving Chicago had already spanned the river upstream.

St. Louis's battle with Chicago took on picturesque rhetorical elements as well. A part-time newspaper man and real estate speculator, Logan U. Reavis, began a campaign in the 1860s to move the nation's capital to St. Louis because of its central location, metropolitan character, and what one optimistic magazine writer called its "healthful climate." In his book, *St. Louis, The Future Great City of the World,* Reavis pointed to the city's location on the fortieth parallel, which he called the "isothermal zodiac." Reavis noted that all great civilizations had grown up on that line, and he predicted that St. Louis would be the center of the next great human civilization. But in the final analysis, railroads, agriculture, and capital had more influence on the fate of nineteenth-century cities than did location on the globe, and Chicago continued to grow because it had the required attributes for metropolitan success.

As they watched their city fall farther behind its neighbor to the north, St. Louis civic leaders spared no opportunity to copy the symbols of the Windy City's success. Exasperated by the defeats suffered by local amateurs at the hands of Chicago's professional White Stockings baseball team, business leader J. B. C. Lucas formed the St. Louis Brown Stockings in 1875. When the Browns beat the White Stockings twice in one day in May 1875, St. Louis newspapers heralded the games as an accurate measure of the relative merits of the two cities. When Chicago won international recognition for its 1893 World's Fair, St. Louis business leaders commenced efforts to stage the 1904 World's Fair in St. Louis. In the long run, neither the baseball team nor the Fair succeeded in besting Chicago's, but even if they had, the fifty-year trends of population and trade in the two cities would not have been altered.

St. Louis's failure to catch up with Chicago raised doubts about the quality of the city's business and political leadership. Doubts that circulated as private opinions for years eventually surfaced as part of a historical interpretation with the 1947 publication of Wyatt Belcher's *Economic Rivalry Between St. Louis and Chicago.* Belcher argued that the shrewd "Yankee" leaders of Chicago invested more aggressively and skillfully than did the conservative "creoles" of St. Louis. As a result, Belcher claimed, the rise of Chicago stemmed directly from the quality of its leaders, and the same could be said about St. Louis's decline.

Belcher's thesis is often utilized as a warning against complacency in St. Louis. Any unwillingness to spend money on new projects—highways, airports, river facilities, or rapid transit—brings a reminder of how conservatism and timidity relegated St. Louis to second place behind Chicago during the nineteenth century. Leadership sometimes does make a difference, but the key development in the rise of Chicago had nothing to do with Creole lethargy or Yankee shrewdness. Some Louisiana French families did enjoy high social status in nineteenth-century St. Louis, but most business leaders came from the same northeastern family backgrounds as did the leaders in Chicago. More than any other single factor, it was the invention of the steel plow that sealed the fate of St. Louis and propelled Chicago into first place in the Midwest.

The site of Chicago had been underdeveloped for years because the prairie farmland near it could not be plowed effectively. Wooden or cast-iron plows worked well enough on prairie sod for one season, but by the next year they became so tangled in the roots of prairie grass that farmers had to spend as much time cleaning their plows as breaking the soil. John Deere, a young man working for the Grand Detour Plow Company in 1837, developed "the plow that scours." It could break the soil, dig through the twelve- to fifteen-inch roots of prairie grass, and remain uncaked by mud and roots. By the time Deere established his own company in Moline, Illinois in 1846, the Illinois prairie was ready for cultivation.

Along with other inventions like the mechanical reaper, Deere's plow enabled Illinois farmers to place under cultivation in only a few decades amounts of land that would have taken previous generations centuries to cultivate. Rich black soil produced abundant yields, stimulating the growth of railroads, farms, and towns throughout central Illinois. Although St. Louis initially received some benefit from this growth, Chicago enjoyed superior access to good farmland and to eastern markets. Blessed by a superior hinterland, lake and rail routes to New York and Boston, and a strategic location for railroad expansion, Chicago quickly moved ahead of St. Louis in population and trade.

By 1860, St. Louis had only fifty thousand more people than Chicago, and by 1870 the city's numerical advantage fell to less than twelve thousand. But dishonest counting in that 1870 census disguised the city's real decline in population, and the reliable 1880 census showed St. Louis with only three hundred fifty thousand inhabitants while Chicago boasted a population of more than one-half million. But the fault did not lie with defects in the isothermal zodiac or with the conservatism of Creole business leaders. Rather, the cause came from something so simple, yet revolutionary, as the invention of the steel plow.

Joseph Weydemeyer:
St. Louis County's Marxist Auditor

Joseph Weydemeyer brought unusual credentials to the job of St. Louis County's auditor at the close of the Civil War. As one might expect, Weydemeyer was known for honesty, intelligence, and hard work; but one might not expect that his preparation for his position in local government included prior service in the Prussian Army, work as a surveyor on New York's Central Park, participation in the anti-slavery movement, experience in the Union Army during the war, a friendship with Karl Marx, and affiliation with the German Communist League.

Born to a wealthy Prussian family in 1817, Weydemeyer began to read socialist literature as a young man. Persuaded that he lived in an unjust society, Weydemeyer resigned his army commission as an artillery officer to become the Cologne representative to the German Communist League. In 1848, he fought for a revolution in Germany, and continued to edit a left-wing newspaper after the revolt failed. When counterrevolutionary forces in Germany began to arrest dissidents, Weydemeyer followed the example of many other German "Forty-eighters" and migrated to the United States.

Weydemeyer settled in New York and became active in that city's emerging labor movement. He edited two German-language journals aimed at working-class immigrants, and he quickly grasped the political realities of his adopted country. Weydemeyer argued that the very existence of slavery undercut the cause of free labor, and he worked ceaselessly to convince white workers that their own futures hinged upon the abolition of slavery. Unlike some in the labor movement who portrayed the slaves themselves as enemies of labor, Weydemeyer insisted that blacks and whites unite along class lines as workers opposed to their common enemies—slave-owners and industrial capitalists.

Weydemeyer led labor opposition to the Kansas-Nebraska Act because of its tacit permission for the extension of slavery into new territories. He looked to the newly founded Republican party as the salvation of the workers. While employed as a surveyor in New York City, he supported Abraham Lincoln for President in the 1860 election. When political hostilities escalated into armed warfare, forty-four-year-old Weydemeyer volunteered for service in the Union Army as an artillery officer, specifically requesting service in Missouri where fighting had already broken out.

Serving as a lieutenant-colonel under General John C. Fremont, Weydemeyer found conditions to his liking in St. Louis. Germans had flocked to the city ever since the 1829 publication of Gottfried Duden's *Report of a Journey to the Western States of North America*, which popularized the region to receptive audiences in Germany. As early as 1837, more than six thousand Germans lived in St. Louis, and more than thirty thousand lived in Missouri. In St. Louis, Weydemeyer discovered a vibrant German-language press, many "Forty-eighters" like himself, and a large and politically aware working class. When his first term of enlistment expired in 1863, he directed his energies toward editing *Neue Zeit* in St. Louis, a publication aimed at increasing support for the war and for the radical Republican candidates who saw the conflict as an opportunity to reshape America along more democratic lines.

In 1864, Weydemeyer returned to the Union Army for a brief stint as commander of the St. Louis district, but politics beckoned once again and he soon left military service to become county auditor. With the defeat of slavery imminent, Weydemeyer believed that true emancipation of labor in both the North and South might be at hand. Freeing the slaves ended one form of oppression, but to Weydemeyer it only underscored the need to end as well the exploitation of factory workers. He reasoned that factory hands producing great wealth for their employers but receiving only a subsistence wage had no more real freedom than slaves.

As a writer for the radical Republican *Westliche Post* and the pro-labor *Daily Press*, Weydemeyer took up the cause of the eight-hour day. In 1865, a mass demonstration by St. Louis workers drew public attention to the demand for shorter hours of labor. All across the country the issue became a hotly contested subject of debate. Reducing work time from ten to eight hours per day may seem like a modest reform to some of us today, but in the nineteenth century it struck at the heart of the postwar industrial system. If workers could ask the state to intervene in the economy to limit the hours of labor, what would prevent them from pursuing political action to change the nature, purpose, pace, or rewards of that labor?

Weydemeyer understood the potential of the eight-hour demand. He knew that its implementation might not change the system very much, at least not at first. But he had high hopes for the process of discussion and debate that would be needed to bring it about. Unlike wage demands, or even grievances about working conditions, the eight-hour demand united all workers around a common goal. Because the movement asked for laws to regulate the hours of work, it had to assume that politics and economics could be combined. To Weydemeyer, that unity and sense of political entitlement contained the seeds of a potential American socialism.

Of course it did not work out that way. The eight-hour demand persisted for another fifty years before it was even tentatively adopted in limited sectors of industry. Weydemeyer died of cholera in the tragic summer of 1866, when that disease once again ravaged St. Louis. He never lived to see the National Labor Union, Knights of Labor, or International Workingmen's Association take up the cause of radical reform in the postwar years. At his death, the man whose fight for social justice had carried him halfway around the world might have seen his life as a failure.

Yet Weydemeyer's influence did not disappear. As labor historian David Roediger observes, the General Strike of 1877 in St. Louis culminated decades of radical political activity. When the city's workers rose up to take control of factories and the city government, they acted in response to the unfilled aspirations and blasted hopes of years of labor and political action. They knew what they wanted in 1877, because they had been prepared for it by years of education and debate dating all the way back to Weydemeyer's time.

Between 1866 and 1877, small victories regulating the hours and wages of workers kept Weydemeyer's vision alive in St. Louis. In the General Strike of 1877, it reappeared with full force. That strike displayed the unity and the focus on political power that Weydemeyer predicted would emerge from the movement for the eight-hour day. When the workers of 1877 went on strike, they acted, at least in part, in response to the writings of St. Louis's Marxist county auditor who warned them that their road would be long, but who also reassured them that in the end it would inevitably curve toward justice.

Virginia Minor: Fighting for Women's Rights

On an October day in 1872, a property-owning, tax-paying, native-born American citizen walked into St. Louis Election District Registrar Reese Happersett's office and asked to be added to the rolls of registered voters. Happersett routinely approved such requests, but not this one. In this case, the prospective voter was a woman, Virginia Minor, and her request challenged established customs and laws that blocked the path to the ballot for women.

Virginia Minor ultimately carried her request all the way to the United States Supreme Court, which ruled against her. But even in defeat, her insistence on equal rights for women publicized the issue and played an important role in the eventual victory of woman's suffrage.

Minor and other St. Louis feminists began their crusade for the vote in the years immediately following the Civil War. They convened in 1867 at the St. Louis Mercantile Library to form an organization committed to that cause. Later that same year they petitioned the state legislature for the right to cast ballots. Although that petition and a subsequent one failed to convince legislators, they opened a battle that would rage for decades.

The Civil War had been an important impetus for their campaign. War requires contributions from every person and tends to foster a sense of equality among those committed to the same cause. The women of St. Louis participated actively in supplying food, supplies, and medicine to the Union Army, and in the process got a taste of public life that they did not wish to give up once hostilities ceased.

In addition, the newly passed Fourteenth and Fifteenth Amendments to the Constitution posed a special dilemma for these women. On the one hand, the amendments guaranteed equal protection of the law to all citizens and the right to vote to male freed men. But by specifically granting rights to male freed men, the amendments also seemed to institutionalize within the Constitution itself the prevailing practice of denying women the right to vote.

Women from all across the United States met in St. Louis in 1869 to discuss these issues. Virginia Minor and her husband, attorney Francis Minor, presented a novel argument to the assembly which they hoped would serve as the basis for the legal challenge to the prohibition against female suffrage. The Minors argued that the Fourteenth Amendment guaranteeing equal protection of the law to all citizens implicitly mandated women's suffrage because only voting guaranteed access to that protection. Virginia Minor noted that women paid taxes just as men did, and she suggested that if men wanted to insist on denying women the right to vote, then maybe they should relieve them of the obligation to pay taxes as well.

When she walked into Reese Happersett's office in 1872, Virginia Minor intended to create a test case for her interpretation of the law. The Registrar denied her request, and the circuit court and the state Supreme Court backed him up. In 1875, the case reached the United States Supreme Court, giving the Minors the opportunity to obtain a definitive ruling on their interpretation of the Fourteenth Amendment.

In their argument before the Court, Virginia and Francis Minor walked a fine line. They cited the sanction given by the Fourteenth and Fifteenth Amendments for federal supervision of state voting qualifications, but the Minors ignored the context of slave emancipation that produced those Amendments in the first place. Similarly they avoided the express mention of male voting rights in the Fifteenth Amendment. They insisted that women either were or were not citizens, and if they were citizens that they could not be denied free and equal access to the exercise of citizenship rights.

As a matter of logic, the argument presented by the Minors made sense, but as a point of law it left the Court unimpressed. The justices ruled unanimously that the states could set qualifications for voting, that women citizens enjoyed equal protection of the law even if they could not vote, and that both custom and law sanctioned an all-male electorate. It would take another forty-four years and a constitutional amendment to change that ruling.

Virginia Minor never lived to see the victory that her case helped initiate. By the time of her death in 1894, the right to vote for women seemed more distant than ever, a victim of male privilege and female disunity. But another war and its attendant social consequences accelerated the pressure for change. Even though a well-financed campaign by big business mobilized conservative women to action against the right to vote because it would be "unfeminine" and would "destroy the family," in 1919 women achieved the victory that Virginia Minor had sought in St. Louis in 1872.

Once women secured the right to vote and began sending their own representatives to state and national legislatures, they began to address the unstated logical extension of Virginia Minor's campaign. The right to vote was not an end in itself, but rather a lever for women to influence the systematic discrimination that closed doors in so many spheres of endeavor. Women and their representatives began introducing legislation in the 1920s demanding that rights guaranteed by the Constitution not be abridged for reasons of gender—in essence the view of the Fourteenth Amendment advanced by Virginia Minor but denied by the Supreme Court.

To this day, women have not succeeded in securing an Equal Rights Amendment to make that principle the law of the land. Like Virginia Minor in the nineteenth century, twentieth-century feminists have had to wage a demeaning struggle—demanding rights that should be their birthright as a matter of course. But their efforts have not been in vain. Like Virginia Minor a century ago, they have reminded their society of the gap between what it professes to be and what it actually is. They have internalized the lesson of Virginia Minor's life, a lesson articulated eloquently by A. Philip Randolph, a freedom fighter in labor and civil rights causes for most of the twentieth century, who said, "Freedom is never granted; it is won" and "Justice is never given; it is exacted." That struggle for freedom and justice for women led by Virginia Minor and those who have followed in her path involves more than the concerns of one gender. Properly understood, it is a struggle *for* everyone that needs to be fought *by* everyone.

The German Language Experiment in the Public Schools: Back to Basics

Few issues in recent memory have divided St. Louisans as sharply as court-ordered busing for racial desegregation of the schools. To its defenders, busing redresses historic inequities in education, countering patterns of deliberate discrimination. But opponents ask why the schools should depart from their primary mission of teaching basic literacy and squander scarce resources on "social engineering." Both sides advocate "quality" education, but each defines the term according to different standards.

The questions raised by busing are not new to St. Louis. One hundred years ago, the same issues about public education, albeit in a slightly different form, dominated civic debate. Then the issue was not busing for purposes of racial integration, but rather German-language instruction to meet the educational needs and cultural desires of a minority group. At that time, St. Louis schools recognized the special circumstances facing German-Americans, and in the process used the educational system to help bring a minority group and its talents and abilities into the mainstream.

Large-scale German migration to St. Louis began during the 1830s, sparked both by political upheaval in Germany and vigorous recruitment in their native land by Missouri German-Americans. By 1840, the German population of St. Louis exceeded five thousand, and many more migrated to the city after the failed German revolution of 1848. Proud of their heritage, these residents asked local newspapers to print German-language columns, and they requested that local schools include German-language instruction in the daily curriculum. Rebuffed on both counts, they attempted to create their own newspapers and schools. In 1860, nine German-language newspapers appeared regularly in St. Louis, and more than five thousand children attended classes conducted exclusively in German, in thirty-eight different private schools. In contrast, only about one-fourth of that number, thirteen hundred children with German parents, attended the public schools, where they made up seventeen percent of the total school population.

Missouri law stipulated that only English could be used in public school classrooms. St. Louis officials cited that prohibition repeatedly when they turned down requests for German-language education. But the Civil War brought a shift in power in the city and the state, which made it possible to consider new alternatives. St. Louis Germans enthusiastically supported the Union side in the war, and they made up an important constituency for the Republican party, locally and nationally. By 1864, St. Louis had a school board willing to defy state law (since a new constitution was certain to be written after the war) and "experiment" with German-language instruction in the public schools.

German instruction started slowly, with only five schools offering classes to some four hundred fifty pupils in 1864. But within ten years, almost fifty percent of the students in St. Louis public schools learned at least part of their lessons in German. The number of German-American children in the public schools climbed from thirteen hundred in 1860 to more than twenty thousand by 1880. In that year, German-language instruction became so popular that almost a quarter of the students in those classes came from non-German families. The "experiment" succeeded in bringing German-Americans into the schools, thereby preventing the formation of a German ethnic ghetto, but it also built an appreciation for German culture among children from other groups.

The period of greatest growth for German instruction in the schools came while William Torrey Harris served as superintendent of schools. One of the nation's leading educational theorists in the late nineteenth century, Harris saw socialization and citizenship as important parts of the schools' mission. He wanted students to learn basic skills and to master the attributes that could make them successful workers, like obedience, punctuality, and self-control. But Harris also worried about the impact of cultural diversity on national character. Too much diversity might leave citizens with no means of communicating with each other; too little might enable one small group to impose their values and beliefs on others.

Harris accepted German-language instruction in the schools, in part because he admired the German language and culture. A Yale graduate with a fondness for the writings of the philosopher G. W. Hegel, Harris had been one of the founders of the *Journal of Spec-*

ulative Philosophy. But his approach to bilingual education went beyond the specific features of German culture. Harris argued that the Germans made up the largest ethnic group in St. Louis, and that a society that did not incorporate their culture into its schools would suffer from social fragmentation. He argued that children from a minority culture might feel under assault if the school forced them to give up their family's language completely. Only by recognizing diversity, he argued, could the school hope to build a unified citizenry.

Not everyone in St. Louis supported German-language instruction in the schools. Irish groups circulated facetious resolutions demanding that Gaelic be taught in the schools, not because they spoke it at home, but because they resented what they viewed as "special privileges" extended to the Germans. Other opponents pointed out that the city did not have French or Hebrew classes, and asked how the school board could justify spending one hundred thousand dollars per year on German-language education for some ten thousand pupils when some schools were overcrowded and on half-day sessions.

By 1887, a combination of successful assimilation, accumulated resentments, and a municipal reform movement that changed the composition of the school board spelled the end for German-language instruction in the public schools. But for twenty-three years, the city had managed to spend large sums of money to make German-American children feel welcome in school and to ease their assimilation into the rest of society.

The special steps taken on behalf of German-American children contrasted sharply with what was offered to African-Americans. The school board barred Negroes from public schools entirely in 1833, and an 1846 state law ordered that "no person shall keep or teach any school for the instruction of Negroes or mulattoes" under penalty of fine and imprisonment. Even when the new state constitution of 1865 mandated public education for Negroes, the city of St. Louis dragged its feet and offered only token schools for black people, using tax dollars paid by black as well as white citizens to fund education for whites only.

Like the German-American parents, blacks struggled to make the schools responsive to their needs. They asked for evening schools, kindergartens, and teacher training institutes, but to no avail. On one occasion, black parents built a school at their own expense, and transferred title to it to the school board in exchange for a promise that the board of education would maintain the building as a school.

The city accepted the building, but then refused to hire black teachers until an organized boycott of the school by parents forced a change of policy. In 1875, St. Louis closed its only high school for blacks—a "school" which met in vacant rooms in an elementary school. Black parents filed a lawsuit demanding that their children be admitted to white high schools, but to preclude that possibility, the school system built Sumner High School and opened it as the first real black high school west of the Mississippi River. Despite above-average attendance among its students, Sumner received the least financial support of any high school. German-American parents could get their language incorporated into the curriculum, but black parents faced a hostile school board that resisted such minor concessions as naming black schools after black historical figures like Crispus Attucks, Toussaint L'Ouverture, and Alexander Dumas.

All-pervasive racism and discrimination in the private sector made the schools an even more important resource for black people than for German-Americans, but the schools offered them less. The *Missouri Republican* summed up the prevailing double standard in 1878 when it argued that assimilation with people of native American or African-American descent "lacked the legitimacy of assimilation with European nationals, especially Germans."

German-language instruction did cost money. It expended precious resources on an "experiment" in human relations. It led to resentments and controversies. It gave to the schools responsibilities for citizenship training rather than just basic education. And it worked. Generations of St. Louisans have profited from the contributions of German-Americans made possible by German-language instruction in the schools in the nineteenth century.

In the 1970s and 1980s, controversies over desegregation and busing once again called attention to the role of education in building citizenship. Once again, social needs attendant to the city's largest identifiable ethnic group created an opportunity for adaptation and ingenuity. The fierce controversy over busing hid other issues—issues of constitutional rights, redress of past wrongs, and the construction of a democratic society. But in the twentieth century, too many St. Louisans chose to squander the talents and resources of the young people who represent the future of the city. Too many supported a segregated and two-class educational system, hoarding resources for the wealthy and skimping on allocations to meet the needs of the poor. Such decisions make a mockery of the labors of William Torrey Harris and others in the nineteenth century in respect to German-language education. They gave St.

Louis a precious gift and are honored today for their hopeful vision of an integrated and pluralistic society. Our own record is less noble, and if we fail, we will earn the contempt of future generations who will wonder why we squandered what we have been given, only to leave the world in far worse shape for those who follow us.

Progressive Baths:
A Watershed in Local History

Between 1907 and 1930, the city of St. Louis built six major baths and several smaller ones in its oldest neighborhoods east of Jefferson Avenue. Bath #1 served the poorest part of the city from its location on Tenth Street between Carr and Biddle. Central European immigrants living near the Anheuser-Busch brewery used the baths near Soulard Market (Bath #2), while a mixture of immigrants and native-born citizens flocked to Bath #3 at Twenty-Third and O'Fallon. Bath #4 at Lucas and Garrison served that neighborhood's predominately black population, although almost all of the baths were open to people of all races. The Buder Bath #5 at Hickory and Ewing still serves as a recreation center for that neighborhood, and Bath #6 at 1120 St. Louis Avenue featured an art deco style. Supplying more than five hundred thousand showers a year in their first decades of operation, the baths remained opened for as many as sixteen hours a day, seven days a week, in order to accommodate the enormous demand for their facilities.

To the working-class population of St. Louis at the turn of the century, public baths represented perhaps the only city institution that directly met their needs. To middle-class reformers, the baths constituted a noble experiment in democracy that could provide slum dwellers with the prerequisites for upward mobility. To the rich, the baths offered a convenient means of improving the public health (and the productivity of workers) without altering the distribution of wealth in society. All but forgotten today, the baths were the measure of civic virtue and well-being to an earlier generation.

Living conditions in St. Louis explained the reasons for the baths' popularity. For years, the local water supply had been associated more with cholera than with cleanliness. Even though efforts to clean it up began in 1866, the city did not have a reliable supply of pure water until 1904. Even in the better neighborhoods during the 1890s, no more than one house in six had indoor plumbing, and poorer sections of town fared much worse. The area bounded by Lucas and O'Fallon between Seventh and Fourteenth streets contained two hundred people for every bathtub. In the alley houses, where one quarter of the city's population resided, there was only one tub for each 2,479 people. The sudden availability of modern bathing facilities run by the city understandably drew an enthusiastic response from (literally) "the great unwashed."

Yet if we can easily understand the popularity of the baths, that still doesn't explain their creation. Why did a city unable to provide adequate food, shelter, or employment for many of its inhabitants choose to provide them with baths? How did a city notorious for its corruption and graft come up with such a seemingly unselfish and generous municipal program? The answers lie in the history of progressivism, that peculiar form of civic optimism so prevalent at the beginning of this century, but so rare today.

The progressives attempted to restore a sense of compassion and social harmony to a city torn by social conflict. They tried to inculcate a sense of social responsibility in the rich and a fidelity to middle-class values among the poor. Their views frequently led them to an unctuous paternalism toward the poor and an overreliance on being useful to the rich, but they still addressed serious social problems in a conscientious manner, and they did initiate many positive reforms.

Public baths gave voice to the most cherished goals of progressivism. In 1906, a city park commissioner hailed institutions like public baths as "educational laboratories in which a conglomerate mass of foreigners of all nationalities develop into stalwart American citizens." A 1911 publication by the Civic League, the most important local progressive organization, made the case in less condescending, but equally urgent terms, presenting the baths as an antidote to the evils of overpopulation, child labor, urban filth, and the demise of the family. The League claimed that "schools and libraries, playgrounds and public baths, by developing their minds, training their bodies, and upbuilding the character of a people, furnish the foundation upon which a nation's welfare depends."

Charlotte Rumbold and Mary McCall founded the St. Louis Civic League and led the campaign for the construction of public baths. Rumbold was a friend and associate of famed Chicago settlement house founder Jane Addams, and a leader of the national public recreation movement, while McCall became well known as a spokesperson for progressive causes all across the country. Rumbold and McCall worked on detailed surveys of housing and health conditions in St. Louis, and they convinced local political and business leaders that a program aimed at eradicating urban blight could be a positive economic asset.

Rumbold and McCall helped start summer playground programs sponsored by the Civic Improvement League and the well-connected members of the elite Wednesday Club. They provided facilities that offered thirty-five thousand showers for needy children in 1902, and their success impelled the city to assume responsibility for the showers by 1904. That year's World's Fair included a municipal exhibit displaying a modern playground and shower to insure that the city's "charity" got the widest possible international notice.

The baths established a good reputation for cleanliness and efficiency. They remained important centers of neighborhood life well into the 1950s, although by that time, transients and truck drivers had become their principle users. For years, the St. Louis Public Schools offered the use of their baths to citizens in poor neighborhoods; the last school to do so—Sigel School, just west of the Soulard neighborhood—discontinued the practice in the late 1970s. Reduced immigration, upward mobility, and urban renewal made the baths increasingly less important as crucibles of American identity, but for most of their history, the baths provided a necessity of life for people otherwise unable to obtain it. In a situation where private housing did not provide adequate numbers of indoor baths, rich and poor alike agreed that it was the city's responsibility to provide what the private sector could not.

It was not until the years following World War II that home bathing became nearly universal in St. Louis. Urban renewal knocked down many older dwellings lacking bathtubs and showers, and new city health and building codes encouraged conversion to indoor plumbing. Federal highway construction and home loan policies addressed the need for better bathing facilities by making it profitable for the private sector to build them in new (and mostly suburban) houses. Yet this privatization of the problem shifted the burdens of payment onto individuals and left far too little assistance available for those with inadequate resources.

The baths remind us of an earlier, and not necessarily inferior, time. They remind us of a day when the rich saw public health expenditures as a wise social investment, when reformers sought to include the poor in the rewards of American abundance, and when poor and working-class people could look to city government for those services and amenities denied to them by the private market. These days, that kind of thinking seems to have gone down the drain.

Muny Opera: Pageantry and Progressivism in the Park

Since 1919, the Muny Opera in Forest Park has offered enjoyment to St. Louisans from all walks of life. Despite the increasing fragmentation of the region's population over five counties on both sides of the Mississippi River, and despite the decline of many other institutions serving the public, the Muny remains one source of entertainment and recreation accessible to a wide variety of citizens. That accessibility is no accident. The people responsible for creating the Muny Opera above all else intended it to serve as a vehicle for bringing people in the city closer together.

Like many other public amenities, the Muny Opera owes its existence to the vision of Charlotte Rumbold and the Civic League. In the early years of the twentieth century, Rumbold wanted to address what she believed to be the major problem confronting St. Louisans—the lack of unity and shared purpose among citizens. To her, the city had become a battlefield where individuals and groups pursued their own selfish interests showing little concern for the common good. She sought to instill a spirit of civic responsibility in rich and poor alike, and to create a common public space that might demonstrate to diverse groups their common stake in society.

Rumbold's analysis emerged from the practical realities of the city. Municipal officials tried to speak of St. Louis as if it were one entity and as if any kind of economic growth would help all residents. In practice, urban economic growth usually involved one group of citizens taking advantage of others, giving rise to innumerable conflicts. The existence of slums created cheap commercial property for businesses, and the value of exclusive residential areas only increased when air or noise pollution made older neighborhoods less desirable. Slumlords profited from overcrowding tenement buildings, and the very existence of slums made middle-class citizens more willing to pay for streetcars taking them to new homes in outlying areas to escape the squalor of the inner city. Under these conditions, it made little sense to speak of unity and shared civic purpose, because the enrichment of some depended upon the impoverishment of others.

Economic conflict promoted political fragmentation. Leaders of both major political parties danced to the tune of the local business elite—"the Big Cinch" as the *Post-Dispatch* called them. Public utilities regularly showed favoritism to big business, as bribery, collusion, and graft became routine methods of commerce. Such behaviors motivated the poor to engage in a corrupt politics of their own. Boss Ed Butler used his control over working-class voters on the near north side to cut deals with the rich that lined his own pockets, but which also secured patronage jobs and other benefits otherwise unavailable to his constituents. It was an age of fragmentation, corruption, and cynicism.

Charlotte Rumbold and the Civic League viewed the pervasive corruption in the city with alarm. As educated middle-class professionals, they had little direct stake in either the corporate rich or the working poor. They saw both classes as selfish and shortsighted. The Civic League instead advanced a spirit of "civic responsibility" that attempted to transcend the pursuit of immediate self-interest that so divided the city. Rumbold campaigned for services for the poor, like playgrounds, public baths, parks, and adult education centers. She argued that all citizens had a stake in developing the city's human capital. She offered the poor an opportunity for assimilation, and she urged the rich to see the dangers of allowing poor people to develop permanent alienation from prevailing social norms.

Yet both the rich and the poor had their doubts about the Civic League's vision of the city. In 1908, the league began a drive to change the city's charter and institute a more "efficient" form of government that would replace many elected officials with supposedly neutral "experts." But what seemed "efficient" or "businesslike" to the league, appeared to workers and small business owners to be a plot to take power out of the hands of the public. The voters rejected the charter reform by more than two to one in a 1911 election, with opposition particularly strong among working-class voters in Irish and German wards.

As they prepared to resubmit their plan for charter reform in 1914, Rumbold and the Civic League searched for a means of encouraging a spirit of cooperation and sacrifice for the common good which they deemed essential to the city's survival. They selected a vehicle that would eventually become the Muny Opera—the Pageant and Masque of 1914. Purportedly a celebration of the 150th anniversary of the city's founding, the Pageant and Masque became the focal point for efforts by the St. Louis Civic League to promote a spirit of mutuality in the local political culture. Eight out of thirteen members on the committee set up to plan the event belonged to the league, and consequently it reflected much of their own point of view. As envisioned by businessman (and chief fund-raiser for the Pageant and Masque) Charles Stix, the goal of the event would be to persuade St. Louisans to care about the city as a whole, not just their own neighborhoods.

Rumbold and her associates wanted to prove that human nature could be used to solve the city's problems, that democracy and progressive values could succeed if only people could unite around their common interests. She recruited the famous dramatists Thomas Wood Stevens and Percy MacKaye to write the script for the pageant and masque respectively, but Rumbold's philosophy permeated its dramatic themes. It noted the contributions of elite first families, but it also argued that the city had not served all of its citizens well.

Organized under the motto "If we play together, we will work together," the Pageant and Masque solicited participation from large numbers of ordinary citizens. Playground associations and settlement houses recruited representatives from diverse European ethnic groups to appear in the performance, and fund-raising efforts included selling souvenir pageant buttons to schoolchildren at a penny apiece as well as soliciting contributions from trade associations and businesses. Staged in Forest Park on the last four days in May, the production enlisted the direct participation of more than seven thousand performers, and it played to more than four hundred thousand spectators in five nights. Spectators sat in seats erected in the natural amphitheatre on Art Hill beneath the art museum. They faced stages erected on pilings sunk into the lagoon below. Each performance offered seating for forty-three thousand spectators, and to make sure that a cross-section of the city's population could attend, twenty-one thousand seats were offered free on a first-come, first-served basis. In addition, tens of thousands crowded together on top of the hill behind the seating areas.

The Pageant played in twilight, from 6:30 to 8:00 P.M. and told the history of St. Louis in allegorical form. It spanned three centuries, moving from Native American settlement to European colonization to the "American" city of the mid-nineteenth century. The Masque began at 8:30 P.M. and presented "the fall and rise of social civilization" in allegorical form. It detailed the fall of the Native American "mound builders'" civilization and the subsequent long battle between the forces of civilization and the forces of gold. In the end of the Masque, St. Louis eventually unites with other cities to enable love, science, and the arts to triumph over gold.

Held less than a month before the referendum vote on the new charter, the Pageant and Masque paved the way for voter approval of the measure in early July. Of course, this success was not just due to the festivities in Forest Park; the League also added provisions for initiative, recall, and referendum to make charter reform more attractive to the voters. But the event fell far short of its goal of uniting all St. Louisans in a common spirit, and for good reason. The administrators of the St. Louis Pageant Drama Association allowed German, Irish, and Anglo-Americans to appear in the drama as St. Louisans, but consigned more recent immigrants to specially designated ethnic roles. Instead of allowing Native Americans to represent themselves, the SLPDA used sixteen gallons of copper-colored make-up to transform white St. Louisans into "Indians" for the performance. Most disgracefully, the Pageant and Masque virtually ignored the forty-four thousand black residents of St. Louis (more than six percent of the total population), erasing their contributions to local history, ignoring them in fund-raising and attendance drives, and casting only a single black man among the seven thousand participants in the drama. In addition, while paying union workers prevailing wages for their work in constructing the site, the Pageant and Masque ignored St. Louis's history of labor productivity and political mobilization.

At the presentations themselves, audiences expressed great enthusiasm for the festive atmosphere engendered by the event, but seemed less than perfectly engaged in the Pageant and Masque's intended message. Noisy vendors sold their wares at the perimeter of the crowd, while animated conversations in the audience frequently drowned out the dialogue coming from the stage. Spectators tore down the fence separating the free seats from the reserved seats on Saturday night, and the security force composed of four hundred fifty police officers, twenty National Guardsmen, and one hundred boy scouts had difficulty controlling the crowds.

Yet the Pageant and Masque served as a great stimulus to many kinds of community theatre in St. Louis. A profit of seventeen thousand dollars enabled the pageant's sponsors to set up the St. Louis Municipal Opera Company and to construct the permanent outdoor amphitheatre that became the site of the Muny Opera.

After a few years of unsuccessful civic theatre, a combination of business interests, eager to have St. Louis considered a first-class city, and cultural leaders, eager to spread a love of the arts throughout the population, combined to form the Municipal Opera with its format of summertime musicals. Rainstorms nearly washed out the opening performances of "Robin Hood" and "The Bohemian Girl" in 1919, but soon the Muny established itself as a viable enterprise.

To be sure, the professional touring companies presenting recycled Broadway shows that now dominate the Muny differ significantly from Charlotte Rumbold's vision of culture as a common lens through which to view the city's experience. St. Louis could still use an honest look at its past and present, and an effort to find common goals, priorities, and a sense of civic responsibility transcending selfish interests. But in the Muny Opera, as well as in the zoo, art museum, libraries, and playgrounds of the city, we continue to see the benefits of the turn-of-the-century vision of Charlotte Rumbold and the Civic League. We may not be so naive as to believe with Rumbold that "if we play together, we will work together," but we can certainly understand that working together mandates a shared sense of the future and a fair distribution of the rewards of growth. The Muny remains a treasured resource on its own merits, but also because it helps keep alive that vision of a shared past, present, and future.

Striking Prose:
The 1936 Federal
Writers Project Strike

Like any industrial center, St. Louis has experienced repeated battles between management and labor. In 1877, wage cuts by the railroads provoked a general strike among workers in different trades who stopped production, seized factories, and took over many of the functions of the city government. In 1900, the refusal of one of the streetcar companies to grant a shorter workday or to reinstate conductors fired for union activities led to a bitter strike marked by pitched battles between residents sympathetic to the strikers and outside scabs hired to break the union. In 1935, workers at Laclede Gas waged a lengthy and dramatic strike for union recognition, printing and distributing their own newspaper as a way of counteracting the promanagement biases of the daily press.

Yet as familiar as they were with strikes, St. Louisans had to be shocked by the picket lines that went up at 408 Olive on October 28, 1936. Instead of auto workers, teamsters, or carpenters, the pickets were writers. The target of their strike was not one of the city's industries, but the federal government. The seventeen strikers manning that day's picket line against the Federal Writers' Project (of the Works Progress Administration) made up one of the most literate picket lines in history. Together they waged St. Louis's most unusual strike.

The federal government set up the writers' project as a response to the depression and as a means of supporting creative artists at a time when even the most commercial of them could not survive on what they earned from publishing. Just as New Deal projects kept alive the talents of artists like Jackson Pollock and Thomas Hart Benton and photographers including Walker Evans and Dorothea Lange, the writers' project supported some of the great figures of recent American literature.

In Missouri, the project featured the talents of Jack Conroy of Moberly, whose novels *The Disinherited* and *A World to Win* remain to this day among the best sources on working-class life during the depression. Along with Jack Balch, Edwa Moser, Hazel Tebeau and others, Conroy devoted his efforts toward assembling a state guide that would accurately reflect the diversity and strength of its culture. Writers appreciated the opportunity to make a living from their art, and they saw the creation of true and useful accounts of local history and culture as fulfilling the highest responsibilities of the creative arts. They did not count on the censorship, political patronage, and outright corruption that were to characterize the administration of the project in Missouri, or on how those factors would eventually force them to go on strike.

The Missouri Democratic party's Pendergast machine made sure that one of its reliable functionaries directed the Federal Writers' Project in the state. Mrs. Geraldine Parker, who had written folk plays and stories about the Ozarks, met with the machine's approval and was placed in charge of the writers' project in Missouri. Under Parker's direction, the project discriminated against blacks, hired whites mainly on the basis of their loyalty to the Pendergast machine, and produced almost no written work despite spending large amounts of money.

Writers who managed to slip through this screening process

encountered direct censorship when they tried to talk about aspects of the state's life and culture that did not fit the Pendergast agenda. Matthew Murray, the state WPA chief and Geraldine Parker's immediate supervisor, deleted references to silicosis-poisoning suffered by the state's lead miners, and he refused to allow the art section of the guide to mention Thomas Hart Benton on the grounds that Murray "wouldn't hang Benton's paintings on the wall of an outhouse."

When the national director of the Federal Writers' Project came to St. Louis, Parker held a dinner in his honor at the Park Plaza Hotel. She demanded that each employee contribute to pay for the dinner, then she neglected to pay the hotel. Wayne Barker, a photographer on the project, found out about Parker's neglect and complained to officials in Washington, D. C. Parker then fired Barker, alleging misuse of photographic equipment and incompetence.

Seventeen writers working on the project went on strike because of Barker's dismissal. They argued that his firing had nothing to do with the charges filed against him, but rather, stemmed from his efforts to form a chapter of the American Writers Union in the office and from his revelations about Parker's financial wrongdoing. They demanded Barker's reinstatement and a twenty percent increase in pay for themselves.

The picket line on October 26, 1936 included Jack Conroy, Edwa Moser, Jack Balch, Hazel Tebeau, six other writers, and two union officials. They carried signs reading "Writers strike for job security" and "Writers must eat," which must have mystified the crowds outside the WPA offices on Fourth and Olive in the heart of the city's financial district. The police, however, understood exactly how they were expected to respond to the pickets. They arrested all seventeen for general peace disturbance. The strikers went to jail proudly, sure that public opinion would help them win the strike. As Jack Balch later told an interviewer, "We felt that we were being patriotic in going on strike, that we were acting in Washington's best interests by opposing the forces in Missouri who were trying to reduce our project to a boondoggle and patronage activity."

Only Conroy remained pessimistic, pointing out that when production workers went on strike their bosses lost money, but that when writers went on strike, the government saved money. Conroy also knew the power of the Pendergast machine in national politics, as well as the willingness of the WPA to sacrifice competence for political advantage.

By December, the strikers had won partial victories with the "resignation" of Parker (who finally paid for the Park Plaza lunch) and with offers of reinstatement for most of the strikers. Barker remained fired, however, and there was no wage increase. Demoralized and defeated, the writers returned to work largely on management's terms.

Under the direction of the Missouri Historical Society's Charles van Ravenswaay and the sponsorship of the state highway department, the state guide eventually reached the public in 1941. It did mention Thomas Hart Benton's painting, spotlighted little-known aspects of folk cultures, and dealt in a reasonably forthright manner with the history of labor in the state. Yet the strikers who forced those changes did not fare as well.

Jack Balch left the WPA and captured his bitter experiences during the strike in a novel *Lamps at High Noon.* Conroy left St. Louis for Chicago, where he collaborated with the great black writer Arna Bontemps on collections of folk tales, a history of black migration to Chicago, and on other works. Conroy felt that he had to leave St. Louis after the strike, explaining: "All of us who came back defeated after the strike were penalized in various ways; and I was put in a much more menial position."

The picket line of writers in October 1936 forms a small part of Conroy's story. But the action by writers to secure better wages, protect their right to join unions, to disclose official wrongdoing, and to use their art to tell the truth about society was more than an oddity of local labor history. It put into action the principles that Conroy and others called for in their writing. Envisioning an art that would bring to life the everyday struggles of ordinary people, Conroy argued "Everything is so confusing and we have so little in the way of precedent or example, we are hampered by cultural deficiencies, we are harried by the fear of unemployment when working and by bodily and mental fatigue. But we have something vital and new to communicate."

You have to suspect that the general strikers in 1877, the transit workers in 1900, and the employees of the gas company in 1935 would have known exactly what he meant.

The Politics of Rapid Transit: Then and Now

Ever since the 1850s, when horse-drawn streetcars took more than ninety minutes to rumble from downtown to the western city limits, St. Louis commuters have been seeking comfortable and convenient transportation. From horse-drawn cars to the electric street railway, from the diesel bus to the superhighway, rapid transit has been an elusive goal for almost a century and a half.

In 1982, the federal Department of Transportation declared its support for a rapid-rail mass transit system with its own right-of-way in St. Louis. Ten years earlier, the local engineering firm Sverdrup Parcel and Associates devised a rapid transit plan in conjunction with the Bechtel Corporation, builders of San Francisco's Bay Area Rapid Transit. In the 1950s, Mayor Joseph Darst recommended a downtown subway system in the abandoned railway tunnels beneath the old post office. The Civitan Club and the board of aldermen endorsed rapid transit in the 1920s in hopes of stimulating downtown commerce and relieving the congestion caused by the appearance of increasing numbers of private automobiles. In 1910, developer E. G. Lewis called for a subway between downtown and University City as an essential part of his plans for that suburb's growth. St. Louis Mayor Rolla Wells pleaded unsuccessfully with the state legislature in 1906 for funds to construct a St. Louis subway, and five separate efforts to build elevated or underground rapid transit systems came to naught in the 1880s and 1890s. City officials once even constructed a concrete pier for elevated tracks at Third and Washington, but the proposed line was never built. All that St. Louis has to show for decades of discussion about rapid transit is a stack of revised and rerevised plans.

The irony of all this planning is that St. Louis actually had an extraordinary rapid transit system between 1890 and 1920 that it lost due to neglect. The electric street railway of that era could take passengers from downtown to the city limits in less than an hour for a fare of five cents. The trip from downtown to Eighteenth Street took only ten minutes, and in another ten the cars reached Grand Boulevard. The majority of the most frequently used streetcar lines ran east and west, but the two with the largest number of daily riders traversed Grand and Jefferson Avenues in a north and south pattern providing extraordinarily convenient transfer connections. Free and universal transfers allowed rides all over the three hundred thirty-four miles of track, and placed most areas of town within easy reach of a large percentage of the population.

An effective interurban railway system on the Missouri Pacific and St. Louis–San Francisco (Frisco) railroad tracks supplemented the electric streetcars. High-speed trains carried passengers from downtown to Kirkwood in thirty-five minutes and to Florissant in

twenty-five minutes. For a basic fare of ten cents, interurbans connected Wellston with St. Charles, downtown with Valley Park and
Creve Coeur Lake. Policies allowing transfers from interurbans to
streetcars made cross-county travel between Florissant and Kirkwood easy and convenient.

The railroads ran five interurban trains daily between Ferguson
and the Wabash Station, nine between Valley Park and Union Station, and twelve between St. Louis and Kirkwood. The diversity of
passengers riding these lines can be gleaned from the nicknames
given to the morning trains from Kirkwood; the 6:00 A.M. train
became known as "the works" because it transported wage laborers, the 7:20 A.M. train was called "the clerks" because it fit the
time schedule of white collar workers, and the 8:00 A.M. train
earned the name "the shirks" because it served those entrepreneurs
and supervisors able to arrive at work after 9:00 A.M.

Before 1891, the city's street railway companies depended mostly
on horse-drawn cars supplemented by a few powered by overhead
running cable. But in that year, the St. Louis Cable and Western
street railway replaced its worn-out cable with electric power lines,
and within a few years all sixty-five of the city's transit lines featured
electric trolleys. Passengers complained of discomfort and waits as
long as ten minutes between cars, but by current standards the
public transportation of 1910 was safe, comfortable, and energy
efficient.

Streetcars also provided important hidden value to the local
economy. The housing density they promoted provided businesses
with a ready supply of neighborhood customers as well as the
ability to attract patrons from other areas. Home builders could use
the availability of public transportation as a lure for buyers in previously undeveloped sections. Factory owners gained access to the
skills of the city's diverse labor pool. Even when private automobiles
began to appear on the streets more frequently in the 1920s, streetcars relieved congestion on crowded city streets by carrying sev-
enty-three percent of rush hour commuters in only eight percent of
the vehicles on the road at that time. In contrast, private automobiles amounted to eighty-nine percent of the vehicles on the
road, but they carried only twenty percent of the passengers.

Electric street railways reached their peak in the early 1920s, and
then waged a losing battle with the automobile for forty years. Some
people simply preferred the convenience and speed of private
transportation, but more important, the automobile's effect on traffic really finished off the streetcar. Parked cars downtown elimi-

nated previously open lanes for traffic, and the resulting congestion caused a logjam of some fifty to one hundred streetcars regularly in the downtown area during rush hour. Sharing the right-of-way between cars and streetcars slowed down public transportation and led to rapid deterioration of the streets. The automobile's very inefficiency—its requirements for gasoline and repairs—made it a profitable item, and vested interests successfully secured indirect subsidies for automobile traffic that were not available for public mass transit.

Mismanagement of streetcar lines also contributed to their demise. Greedy monopolists immersed in civic corruption controlled the electric railway lines. They plundered the public in any number of ways, ranging from misuse of capital to bribing public officials. Yet even honest and efficient managers might have had trouble making a success out of rapid transit as a private business in St. Louis for very long. The large number of streetcar lines before 1900 encouraged wasteful duplication; companies built lines they didn't need merely to keep competitors out of certain areas. Civic legislation mandating three blocks in between lines proved unenforceable, and when the companies consolidated into a single streetcar company, the resulting jumble of unplanned and often unneeded tracks had to be maintained because home buyers had followed the tracks into new areas of development. The consolidated company cut service to cut its losses, thereby increasing the demand for automobile or motorbus traffic that then further weakened the streetcars as a viable means of transportation.

The widely-dispersed development encouraged by the rise of the streetcar also created serious social problems. Citizens welcomed the chance to escape deteriorating inner city neighborhoods for the fresh air, open space, and new homes of the suburbs, but that movement created problems. Old areas fell into neglect, abandoned neighborhoods became new slums, and each decline in inner city property values spurred additional westward development, which in turn increased the costs of commuting. Streetcar lines insured the success of suburbs like University City and Clayton, but they damaged the quality of life within the city limits.

As historian Sam Bass Warner observes in his important book *Streetcar Suburbs*, suburbanization led to greater residential segregation by class. The old inner city had many problems, but its mixture of rich and poor in close proximity contributed to a unified and rich community identity. Suburbs stratified the city by class, encouraging privatism and a focus on immediate family needs at the expense of civic responsibilities. Suburbs made use of metropolitan resources like water, sewer, and utility services, but they made little contribution to the center city's economic, cultural, or political welfare. As community problems increased, streetcar suburbs encouraged St. Louisans to seek private individual escapes rather than collective public solutions to common problems.

Ironically, the rise of the private automobile also held open the possibility of ending that community fragmentation. Cars provide so much individual mobility that they might encourage less dense settlement and less class and racial segregation in neighborhoods. But the automobile's transformation from a luxury to a necessity took place in cities already defined by the imperatives of the streetcar, by the class and racial fragmentation which remained essential components of automobile-related suburban growth in the 1940s, 1950s, and 1960s.

Now that higher energy costs and declines in consumer purchasing power threaten the commuter's access to inexpensive automobile transportation, the time might be right for rapid transit after all. It could connect business centers downtown to those in Clayton; it might move workers to new jobs and help bring the region closer together physically and spiritually. But transportation can only take riders from place to place. Without decent housing for all citizens and without a common sense of public space and civic responsibility, St. Louis's next rapid transit system may be no more successful than the one it had, and lost, at the turn of the century.

Conclusion
The Poetics and Politics of Place

St. Louis owes its existence to circumstances of space, to the physical features of its terrain and location. Both Native Americans and Europeans selected it as a site for settlement because its bedrock limestone resists erosion from the powerful currents of the Mississippi, and its bluffs minimize the risks of excessive flooding while still allowing access to the river. Located in the middle of the continent and served by one of the largest systems of navigable waterways in the world, St. Louis enjoys proximity to rich farmlands and abundant iron ore and coal deposits. Whatever their other differences, the city's Native American, Spanish, French, British, and American inhabitants have all based their settlements on the seeming certainties of place in St. Louis.

Yet human uses of places can transform their meanings. To Mississippian Indians, burial mounds, perhaps including Sugar Loaf Mound in south St. Louis, represented sacred ground, but to nineteenth-century developers, they constituted only an obstacle to development. One of St. Louis's most prominent families first developed the land on Biddle Street as an exclusive area guaranteeing privacy for the rich who built homes there, but over the years, the street became an embodiment of cultural pluralism and the locus of powerful movements for social justice. Before the invention of the self-scouring plow, St. Louis could boast the best location in the nation for the distribution of agricultural products. But once John Deere's invention opened up for cultivation the prairies of Illinois, Chicago had obvious geographical advantages over St. Louis. The land itself did not change, but its social meaning did.

It is necessary to dig beneath the surface, literally and figuratively, to comprehend the secrets of St. Louis. Few people know that over the centuries, acidic water has seeped down into St. Louis's bedrock, dissolving the limestone and carving large fissures for underground streams, rivers, and caverns. Underground springs run through the basements of the public library, the Missouri Pacific Building and the old post office, and a complicated labyrinth of grottos, caves, and tunnels lies beneath the city streets. For much of

121

the city's history, this subterranean reality has helped shape activities that take place on the terrain above the ground.

Caves beneath the earth provided a kind of natural cooling that enabled nineteenth-century German-American brewers in St. Louis to make beer in the summertime, a luxury in the days before the invention of refrigeration. Underground mines in Forest Park and throughout the city provided most of the coal used to heat residences during the nineteenth century. Seams of clay under the Hill provided employment opportunities for the Italian immigrant miners and craftsmen who settled there, as well as producing raw materials for the city's clay and firebrick industries. The brick and terra-cotta buildings that dominate the architecture in the older sections of St. Louis testify to the abundance of these building materials deep in the St. Louis soil.

Even recreation has responded to the opportunities under the St. Louis earth. Joseph and Ignatz Uhrig purchased land in 1849 at the corner of Jefferson and Washington that included entry to an underground cave, which they built into an entertainment showplace. Connected by an underground narrow-gauge railroad to the Uhrig Brewery, Uhrig's Cave offered customers beer, food, and first-class musical entertainment in cool comfort forty feet below street level. In 1947, Lee Hess rediscovered a cave beneath the old Lemp Brewery at Thirteenth and Cherokee Streets, widened the entrance, and opened it as "Cherokee Cave," a tourist and educational site. Most of the entrances to these caves have been closed, and some St. Louisans live their whole lives without knowing they are there. But they have shaped the physical appearance and the cultural history of St. Louis in important ways.

Looking beneath the surface of St. Louis's cultural geography reveals significant subterranean currents of history and culture that have played a hidden role in shaping the city's identity. It can also serve as a metaphor for what I have tried to do in this book, to look beneath the surface and connect the visible appearances of the city to forgotten underground currents and influences. Just as the presumed stability of bedrock limestone is belied by the fissures and caverns beneath its surface, the seeming certainties of place that define St. Louis become destabilized and problematized once you dig deeply enough.

My approach is to insist upon both the absolute importance and the ultimate irrelevance of place. To be sure, the particularities of place in St. Louis provide crucial evidence about how the city has been shaped by circumstance, context, and contingency. Understanding the power of place can illumine important aspects of the past and present. But places have no destiny of their own; they are always shaped by human activity. Humans are sociable and interdependent. The story of any one place ultimately involves connections to other places. Too much of a foundational commitment to the unique and singular attributes of one locality can obscure, rather than illumine, relevant issues of context. It can substitute parochial boosterism for careful and creative analysis.

St. Louis has been the site of exciting and inspiring innovations in urban life, like public baths, German language instruction in the public schools, and the Muny Opera, but it has also been a place where Native Americans and African-Americans were held as slaves and where immigrant labor was exploited. There is nothing inherently noble or ignoble in the place; to the contrary, only the actions of human beings have ennobled or degraded it.

Stories about place in St. Louis are also often stories about displacement. Conquest, trade, and migration have moved people from one locality to another; only rarely in the modern world can humans ground themselves and their ancestors in one spot on the globe. Instead, residence in any given location includes memories of a previous home and perhaps a future destination. Places become important not so much for what they have always been, but for the currents that flow through them at any given moment, for the creative cultural adaptations and innovations that connect people to one another. Scott Joplin and Theodore Dreiser came from other cities to make contributions to St. Louis history, but they also took parts of their St. Louis experiences with them elsewhere to fashion an art with international influence. Kate Chopin and Josephine Baker were both born and raised in St. Louis, but had to leave to find their true callings and to receive appropriate recognition. Some of St. Louis's most important institutions, like Homer G. Phillips Hospital, the Turnvereins, and the Polish Falcons lodge grew out of the agonies and aspirations of immigrants and the descendants of slaves. The people who built those institutions rarely saw their names in the newspapers, much less on buildings or statues, but their labor built the city, and their efforts to secure a better life for themselves often produced extraordinary benefits for others. In *Redburn*, Herman Melville wrote that if you spill a drop of American blood you spill the blood of the whole world. Similarly, if you look closely at the history and culture of an American city you discover the history and culture of the whole world.

For example, Heinrich Boernstein's popular 1851 dime novel, *The*

Mysteries of St. Louis, blended anti-slavery, anti-capitalist, and deeply prejudiced anti-clerical views into a lurid terror-filled tale that reflected both the values of German-American immigrant intellectuals and the popular reading tastes of the time. The book made frequent references to St. Louis locations and personalities as it unfolded its melodramatic mystery tale. But it reached German-speaking audiences on both sides of the Atlantic, making life in St. Louis an organic part of German popular culture while reading the St. Louis experience from a decidedly German perspective. Part of Germany lived on in St. Louis, not just in the accomplishments of exceptional individuals like Joseph Weydemeyer, but in the tone and texture of everyday life as represented so carefully in *The Mysteries of St. Louis.*

To think of St. Louis as a part of Germany or of Germany as a part of St. Louis raises questions about our concept of local identity. From its earliest days, St. Louis existed in relation to an international world system. The internal crises of France, England, and Spain brought European settlers into conflict with Mississippian Indians, and the Native Americans had to adjust their culture to European demands almost immediately on contact with them. Global struggles for empire shaped the contours of the local St. Louis economy from the start, and the city became part of the United States because of the Toussaint L'Ouverture rebellion in Haiti, not because of any decisions made locally.

In the nineteenth century, St. Louis business leaders pinned their hopes on an expanding international economy. Missouri Senator Thomas Hart Benton identified trade with China as essential to St. Louis's well-being as early as the 1840s. The products that passed through St. Louis ports before the Civil War served an economy dependent on slave labor. Such a labor force had to be kidnapped from Africa by European and American merchants. As a regional production and distribution center, St. Louis exerted a profound influence on the American Southwest, serving as a supply and service center to American settlers headed for Spanish and later Mexican land. Thus local identity in St. Louis emerged in the context of the city's place in world affairs, in dialogue with the politics of Europe, Asia, Africa, and Latin America.

It should not be surprising, then, that crises in the rest of the world frequently manifested themselves in St. Louis, if only in microcosm, as the case of Ricardo Flores Magon demonstrates. In 1905, Magon and his brothers, Enrique and Jesus, published the founding documents of the Mexican Liberal Party in a three-story tenement at 107 North Channing Avenue near the Mill Creek Valley. The Magon brothers had begun publishing a weekly newspaper, *Regeneracion*, in Mexico City in 1900, but had been forced to leave Mexico for Texas because of political persecution by the corrupt dictatorial regime of Porfirio Diaz. When Diaz's agents continued to harass them they transferred their operations further north to St. Louis, where they thought they would be safe. In St. Louis they encountered European immigrants and native-born workers committed to radical social change.

From the slum building on North Channing Avenue, Magon and a small group of fellow exiles from Mexico published his newspaper with its impassioned advocacy of political reform, the eight-hour day, and the abolition of debt slavery. His efforts led to the formation of the first Mexican trade unions and ultimately to the 1910–1911 Mexican Revolution. But in St. Louis, collaboration among postal authorities, agents of the Diaz government, and two St. Louis detective agencies—Furlong's Secret Service Company at Eighth and Olive and Pinkerton's Agency at Seventh and Chestnut—led to the arrest of three of the editors of *Regeneracion* on charges that their publication had libeled an associate of President Diaz. With the newspaper's editors jailed, St. Louis police detectives ransacked their offices on North Channing Avenue and confiscated their printing press. Even worse, the officers impounded *Regeneracion*'s subscription list and turned it over to the Mexican consul, who sent it back to Mexico for use in imprisoning hundreds of Mexican liberals. While free on bond, the defendants learned that the Mexican government sought to have them extradited for alleged crimes committed in Mexico. Certain that Diaz would have them put to death, Magon and his comrades skipped out on their bail and fled from the authorities. Eventually the United States government captured Magon, charged and convicted him of violating American neutrality laws, and imprisoned him in Leavenworth, Kansas, where he died in 1922. The incident represented only a tiny chapter in the history of political harassment in St. Louis, but it had important consequences for the revolution and the cause of social reform in Mexico.

When the Magon brothers tried to evade the snares set up by local authorities, or when a small colony of Chinese immigrants gathered in a "Chinatown" community just south of downtown, or when large numbers of Bohemian, Croatian, and black migrants moved to St. Louis to work in its factories, many residents from long-established families voiced open disdain for the newcomers and the ways in which their presence transformed the local community. But of course, these "first families" themselves displaced the native American inhabitants of the area, and they actively participated in an economic system that sought to tap the human and material resources of Latin America, Africa, and Asia for their own benefit. Backers of the 1904 St. Louis Olympic Games and of the World's Fair hoped that their efforts would spread the reputation of St. Louis around the globe, but centuries of trade, imperial struggles, and immigration had already firmly established St. Louis as part of the international economy and the world community.

Yet for all its global connections, some of St. Louis's proudest moments have come from extremely short journeys within the city limits. When Virginia Minor walked into the registrar's office to seek the vote for women in 1872, or when employees of the Federal Writers Project left their offices to go on strike in 1936, they took important steps for justice and human dignity. When Billy Peek found his way to the blues clubs of East St. Louis or when Bix Beiderbecke mixed together the musics he heard at the St. Louis Symphony, the Arcadia Ballroom, and the Chauffeurs Club, these musicians crossed imposing boundaries dividing races and classes. They could not have acted without the benefit of the particular and specific political culture of St. Louis, but their actions would have had little meaning had they not addressed conditions of national and international significance.

My own understanding of St. Louis has come from both long journeys and small steps. My train trip halfway across the country in 1963 brought me into an aging and nearly empty Union Station. A taxi cab took me west through the Mill Creek Urban Renewal Area which the driver described to me as "Hiroshima Flats." During my first summer in the city I visited the Gaslight Square entertainment district, where the St. Louis Ragtimers introduced me to the music of Scott Joplin, and Singleton Palmer's bands presented a distinctly St. Louis version of Dixieland jazz. In old neighborhoods throughout the city—LaSalle Park, Soulard, and Hyde Park—I marveled at the brick and terra-cotta row houses with their magnificent ornamentation and craftwork. That summer I visited the General Motors Factory at the corner of Union and Natural Bridge. Now, almost thirty years later, Union Station is a shopping mall and the Mill Creek Area remains devastated. Boarded-up abandoned buildings are all that remain of Gaslight Square. The General Motors Plant has closed, and the ten thousand jobs it offered have been moved elsewhere.

In 1973, the Pruitt-Igoe housing project, where I had participated in voter registration projects in the 1960s, had so deteriorated that the city had it dynamited and destroyed. When I worked with rank-and-file dissidents in Teamsters Local 688 in the early 1970s, we used to pass out leaflets during shift changes at the factory gates of Wagner Electric, American Car Company, Scullin Steel, National Steel, and Carter Carburetor. Today those factories are all closed. The local auto industry alone lost ten thousand jobs between 1979 and 1980. Manufacturing employment in the St. Louis area dropped by forty-four thousand jobs between 1979 and 1982 as unemployment rose above eleven percent. The entire St. Louis area has lost population, the central city most of all. Politicians, newspaper editorialists, and urban affairs experts tell us that the city has been sick, suffering from blight and decay. But that diagnosis is a dangerous one. Over the years the "cure" for this decay has always been to take the property and destroy the communities of the poor to build heavily subsidized office buildings and commercial centers for the elite. More harm has been done by the "cure" than by the "disease." While the emergence of redevelopment projects and new jobs provides optimism about the city to investors and politicians, the industrial economy that provided opportunities for upward mobility and produced a large wage-earning middle-class population is gone forever and so are many of the vital neighborhoods, community services, and shared public spaces that gave the city its distinctive texture and tone.

I don't pretend that the places that I knew were all wonderful. The old neighborhoods had many problems, and the city's industrial base meant pollution, injuries on the job, and arduous labor for many workers. My understanding of cities is that people and places and politics come and go; change is inevitable and necessary. But what remains is the legacy of what people do for one another, or *to* one another. Above all, that is where the history of St. Louis has something important to teach us. What seems to have been lost, along with the old neighborhoods and landmarks and factories, is the sense of mutuality and negotiation established over the years by people who learned to live with one another. The increasing fragmentation of St. Louis, its increased polarization between the races, its stratification of classes, and the segmentation of its housing and labor markets squanders the public resources painstakingly built over the years to accommodate different interests and needs. As public space downtown increasingly becomes colonized by private profit-making interests, services crucial to the whole population, like schools, libraries, health care, and housing, remain criminally underfunded.

I no longer live in St. Louis; I no longer expect to live there ever again. But it still seems like home to me, more so than Paterson, New Jersey in which I was raised, or than any of the cities in Texas, Massachusetts, California, and Minnesota in which I have lived. When I hear Chuck Berry's music, when I read the sports pages to see how the Cardinals are doing, when hot summer days remind me of north St. Louis barbecues and south St. Louis beer gardens, of rowing in Forest Park and of float trips on the Meramec River, I recognize my connections to the city. Every time I visit, I find that something else has changed, not just in the built environment but in the people that I knew. And of course I change too. But some things do not change. Because of my years in St. Louis, I know something about people and places and politics; about how power works and how people resist it. I know how imagination and desire work to transform physical space, and how people come to learn that they have common interests and needs. It is not a function of the place itself, but of people and what they have to offer, their capacities for adaptation and change, their creative adjustments to circumstances not of their own making. Place, by itself, has no redemptive properties, but people do.

When we write about cities, only incidentally do we confront their geographies, built environments, and political institutions. Ultimately we write about cities because we need to rewrite and rethink and revise our relationships with other people. The blues singer Lonnie Johnson understood this. He recorded and played in St. Louis for many years. Like many of us, he learned much from the city and its people. By being firmly grounded in one place, he learned important things about everyplace. When asked about the inspiration for his music, Johnson replied with some thoughts that might well serve as a guide for how we think about cities—their pasts, their presents, and their futures:

> I sing blues. My blues is built on human beings on land. See how they live, see their heartaches and the shifts they go through with love affairs and things like that—that's what I write about and that's the way I make my living. It's understanding others, and that's the best I can tell you. My style of singing has nothing to do with the part of the country I comes from. It comes from my soul within.

Bibliographic Essay

Historians attempt to fashion coherent narratives about the past on the basis of those records that survive in the present. Not everything that happens gets written down. Not all written documents get saved. With social and cultural history especially, historians attempt to recreate the rich diversity of everyday life experiences in the past on the basis of the most minute fragments of evidence.

When writing the history of St. Louis, our sources are especially limited. Compared with cities of similar size and importance, the archival records for St. Louis are rather slight. The local educational institutions, historical societies, and newspapers have done a poor job of collecting and preserving information about St. Louis history. Their holdings that deal with the dominant economic and political institutions in the city are respectable enough, but too little of their collections concern the everyday life experiences of ordinary people. As a result, much of what we should know about St. Louis's past remains yet to be collected from oral history, folklore, and material culture studies that have not yet begun. Recent efforts by curators at the education department of the Missouri Historical Society and by library archivists at the University of Missouri–St. Louis and Washington University provide grounds for optimism about the direction of local history studies, but without major commitments of resources by public and private agencies, our knowledge about the St. Louis past will remain more tentative and speculative than it should be.

In this book, I have based my interpretations of St. Louis history largely on evidence from published sources, but archival and manuscript collections have been helpful on some topics. The Jefferson National Expansion Memorial Archives at the Gateway Arch contain useful information about the Mississippi waterfront and levee, westward expansion, and riverfront urban renewal, including the construction of the Arch. The Missouri Historical Society has extensive holdings on diverse subjects including French and Spanish colonial rule, and the 1904 Louisiana Purchase Exposition. The St. Louis University Archives and Oral History Center features oral histories on ethnic history, the Great Depression, and the New Deal. The University Archives and Research Collection at Southern

Illinois University at Edwardsville includes the papers of labor leader Harold Gibbons. The Western Historical Manuscripts Collection at the University of Missouri–St. Louis contains important papers about labor and socialist activism, especially in the papers of David T. Burbank, Ernest Calloway, the International Ladies Garment Workers Union, Paul Preisler, and the Socialist party. The University Archives and Research Collection at Washington University includes the papers of St. Louis Mayors Kaufman, Tucker, Cervantes, Poelker, and Conway, and of businesses, including Harland, Bartholomew & Associates, Sverdrup-Parcel, and the St. Louis Car Company, as well as the Chamber of Commerce, Civic Progress, and the Urban League.

The best secondary source on St. Louis history is James Neal Primm's *The Lion of the Valley* (Boulder, Colorado: Pruett Publishing, 1981). Primm's bibliography is an excellent guide to archives, manuscripts, and scholarly materials on St. Louis history, and his text is an exceedingly reliable, comprehensive, and knowing interpretation of the city's past. Primm's chronology is also exceedingly useful as a guide to research in back issues of the *St. Louis Post-Dispatch*, *St. Louis Globe-Democrat*, and *St. Louis Argus*.

My research on places in St. Louis's past drew upon the sources listed above as well as James Neal Primm, "Locational Factors in the Development of St. Louis," *Gateway Heritage*, 10–16; Robert Kerr, "Cahokians Built a Great City but Left Few Clues To Puzzle," *St. Louis Post-Dispatch* (January 3, 1991): 29; Donald E. Pienkos, *One Hundred Years Young: A History of Polish Falcons in America* (New York: Columbia University Press, 1987); Gary Mormino, *Immigrants on the Hill* (Urbana: University of Illinois Press, 1986); James Francis Robinson, "The History of Soccer in the City of St. Louis," Ph.D. dissertation, St. Louis University, 1966; John Kasson, *Amusing The Million* (New York: Hill and Wang, 1978); Roland Binz, "German Gymnastic Societies in St. Louis, 1850–1913: Emerging Socio-Cultural Institutions," Master's thesis, Washington University, 1983; Susan Waugh McDonald, "Edward Gardner Lewis: Entrepreneur, Publisher, American of the Gilded Age," *Bulletin of the Missouri Historical Society*, 35: n. 3, pp. 154–63; Sidney Levi Morse, *The Siege of University City* (St. Louis: University City Publishing Company, 1912); University City Public Library, Edward G. Lewis Collection; Katherine Corbett, Missouri's Black History From Colonial Times to 1970," *Gateway Heritage*, 4: n. 1, pp. 16–25; John T. Clark Files, Urban League Collection, Washington University Libraries Special Collections.

Information on people in St. Louis history comes from Stephen Reiss, *City Games* (Urbana: University of Illinois Press, 1989); Gregg Lee Carter, "Baseball in St. Louis, 1867–1875: An Historical Case Study in Civic Pride," *Bulletin of the Missouri Historical Society*, 31: n. 4; David Voigt, *American Baseball* (Norman: University of Oklahoma Press, 1966); the Kate Chopin Papers at the Missouri Historical Society; Emily Toth, "St. Louis and the Fiction of Kate Chopin," *Bulletin of the Missouri Historical Society*, 32: n. 1, pp. 33–50; Bonnie Stepenoff, "Freedom and Regret: The Dilemma of Kate Chopin," *Missouri Historical Review*, 81: n. 4, pp. 447–66; *Missouri Historical Society*, 31: n. 4; Theodore Dreiser, *A Book About Myself* (New York: Boni and Liveright, 1922); Richard Lingeman, *Theodore Dreiser* (New York: Putnam, 1966) and *At the Gates of the City, 1871–1907* (New York: G.P. Putnam's Sons, 1986); David Thelen, *Paths of Resistance* (New York: Oxford University Press, 1986), 117–29; James Haskins, *Scott Joplin: The Man Who Made Ragtime* (Garden City, New York: Doubleday, 1978); Rudi Blesh and Harriet Janis, *They All Played Ragtime* (New York: Oak Publishing, 1966); David Jasen and Trebor Jay Tichenor, *Rags and Ragtime* (New York: Dover, 1989); Lynn Haney, *Naked at the Feast* (New York: Dodd and Mead, 1981); Phyllis Rose, *Jazz Cleopatra* (New York: Doubleday, 1989); Congress of Racial Equality Papers, State Historical Society, Madison, Wisconsin; Harriet Ottenheimer, "The Blues Tradition in St. Louis," *Black Music Research Journal*, 9: n. 2, pp. 136–39; W. C. Handy, *Father of the Blues: An Autobiography* (New York: MacMillan, 1941); Ralph Berton, *Remembering Bix* (New York: Hamerow, 1974); Katharine T. Corbett and Mary E. Seematter, "No Crystal Stair: Black St. Louis 1920–1940," *Gateway Heritage*, 8: n. 2, pp. 8–15; Interview with Billy Peek, Oral History Collection, Western Historical Manuscripts Collection, University of Missouri–St. Louis.

Sources on politics include C. L. R. James, *Black Jacobins* (New York: Random House, 1989); Steven Rowan and James Neal Primm, *Germans for a Free Missouri: Translations from the St. Louis Radical Press, 1857–1862* (Columbia: University of Missouri Press, 1983); Paul Buhle, Mari Jo Buhle, Dan Georgakus, editors, *Encyclopedia of the American Left* (New York: Garland, 1990); David Roediger, "Not Only the Ruling Classes to Overcome, but Also the So-Called Mob: Class, Skill, and Community in the St. Louis General Strike of 1877," *Journal of Social History*, 19: 213–39. David Roediger and Philip Foner, *Their Own Time* (Chicago: Charles Kerr, 1989); Laura Staley, "Suffrage Movement in St. Louis During the 1870s," *Gateway Heritage*, 3: n. 4; Monia Cook Morris, "The History of Women Suffrage in Missouri," *Missouri Historical Review,* v. 25 (October) 1930, 67–82; Sara Evans, *Born for Liberty* (New York: Free Press, 1989); Selwyn Troen, *The Public and the Schools: Shaping the St. Louis System, 1838–1920* (Columbia: University of Missouri Press, 1975); Sister Audry Olson, "The Nature of an Immigrant Community in St. Louis: St. Louis Germans 1850–1920," *Missouri Historical Review;* William Torrey Harris Papers at Missouri Historical Society; Katharine T. Corbett and Mary E. Seematter, "Black St. Louis at the Turn of the Century," *Gateway Heritage,* 7: n. 1, pp. 41–47; Donald Bright Oster, "Nights of Fantasy: The St. Louis Pageant and Masque of 1914," *Bulletin of the Missouri Historical Society,* 31: n. 3, pp. 175–205; David Glassberg, "To Explain the City to Itself" in his book *American Historical Pageantry* (Chapel Hill: University of North Carolina Press, 1990), Caroline Loughlin and Catherine Anderson, "Forest Park: More People, More Uses (1885–1901)," *Gateway Heritage,* 7: n. 3, pp. 26–33; Monty Penkower, *The Federal Writers Project: A Study in Government Patronage of the Arts* (Urbana: University of Illinois Press, 1977); Jerre Mangione, *The Dream and the Deal: The Federal Writers Project, 1935–1943* (Boston: Little, Brown & Co., 1972); Missouri Highway Department, *Missouri: A Guide to the Show-Me State* (New York: Duell, Sloan and Pearce, 1941); John C. Bollens, *Exploring the Metropolitan Community* (Berkeley: University of California Press, 1961); June Wilkinson Dahl, *A History of Kirkwood, 1851–1965* (Kirkwood, Missouri: Kirkwood Historical Society, 1965); Kenneth Jackson, *Crabgrass Frontier* (New York: Oxford University Press, 1985).

Material in the conclusion comes from Helen D. and Joseph Vollmar, Jr., "Caves, Tunnels and other Holes . . . under St. Louis," *Gateway Heritage,* 8: n. 2, pp. 1–7; Bernard Axelrod, "St. Louis and the Mexican Revolutionaries, 1905–1906," *Bulletin of the Missouri Historical Society,* v. 28: n. 2, pp. 94–107; Michael Denning, *Mechanic Accents* (London and New York: Verso, 1987); Henry Boernstein, *The Mysteries of St. Louis* (Chicago: Charles H. Kerr, 1990).

Index